Y0-DNK-934

When Your Heart
is Broken

Jesus is Lord!

Walter Albritton, SJC

By Walter Albritton

When Your Heart is Broken

Jesus can turn the tears of failure

into the wine of victory

By Walter Albritton

More Praise for "When Your Heart is Broken"

"All of us who are guests on planet earth will experience the deaths of loved ones and face physical, emotional or spiritual difficulties. Walter Albritton has been there. He teaches us how hardship can help us mature spiritually."

The Rev. J. Richard Peck, Director of Communications
General Commission on United Methodist Men

"Walter's writing means so much to so many. This book will strengthen your faith in our Lord Jesus Christ. Thank you Walter!"

Cecil Spear, Retired Civil Engineer

"I know thousands of ministers but none that lives what they preach more profoundly than Walter. His words flow out of his experience with life's brokenness and guide us with wisdom toward hope and recovery. I gladly recommend this book."

Vaughn Stafford, Lead Pastor
Clearbranch United Methodist Church, Trussville, AL

"Walter is a gifted writer and more importantly a real man of God. I have read many of his books and recommend this one. It is one of Walter's best. Any person who reads it will be blessed."

Jere L. Beasley, Principal & Founder, Beasley Allen

"This book will inspire you to look beyond the layers of your broken and disappointed heart and see the Lord's unfailing love for you! He does give beauty for ashes! I found myself writing down quotes from this book and putting them on my mirror!"

Jennifer Aughtman
Director of Children's Ministry, Saint James UMC

More Praise for "When Your Heart is Broken"

"On Christmas morning last year my husband and best friend suffered a heart attack and died suddenly. There is no way to describe how broken and lost I felt. But Christmas was Jay's favorite day of the year and I knew I had to choose not to live in the darkness of my loss. Walter says we can choose the color of our brokenness and I did that; I chose the colors of hope, joy and love. This book is filled with stories that invite us to remember precious things – a hearty laugh, a forgiving spirit, a passion for the Lord. God, our DAD, cherishes his children and wants the best for us. Believing that we can affirm with Walter that 'Joy can laugh at sorrow for joy will have the last word.' Hallelujah!"

Jennifer Andrews, Montgomery, Alabama

Copyright © October, 2014 By Walter Albritton

Cover design and book compositing by Susan Heslup

ISBN – 13: 978-1502472380

ISBN – 10: 1502472384

Copies of this book may be ordered from:
www.Amazon.com
Or
Christian Bookstores

Or by sending an email to:
walbritton@elmore.rr.com

Copyright, October, 2014
By Walter Albritton

All Scripture quotations are from the New International Version unless otherwise noted.

All rights reserved. No part of this publication may be reproduced, stored in a retrieval system, or transmitted in any form or by any means, electronic, mechanical, photocopying, recording, or otherwise without the prior permission of the publisher.

To

Neva Caroline Williams

Margie Helen Flomer

Seth Henry Albritton

Pearl Albritton

My sisters, my brother and his wife,
faithful disciples of Jesus
who have refused to let brokenness
have the last word

Introduction

"THE LORD IS CLOSE TO THE BROKENHEARTED
AND SAVES THOSE WHO ARE CRUSHED IN SPIRIT."
– PSALM 34:18

Everyone eventually experiences the agony of a broken heart. Then in the midst of pain and heartache a difficult choice must be made – whether to sit in misery and whine or trust God for healing and recovery.

I have drunk the bitter dregs of brokenness. I have felt the urge to give up and sink into the abyss of defeat. I have fought the numbness of despair. But in every dark night the Lord Jesus has come with tender forgiveness and lifted me out of the pit. He has taken me by the hand and helped me to my feet. He has invited me to let him help me walk on. I have accepted his offer many times so I know firsthand there is hope for the brokenhearted. I have felt His presence in my brokenness and more than once he has saved me when my spirit was crushed. I discovered that the One who turned water into wine could change the tears of my failure into the wine of victory. Only then was I able to affirm the words of Isaiah 41:10 for myself:

So do not fear, for I am with you;
do not be dismayed, for I am your God.
I will strengthen you and help you;
I will uphold you with my righteous right hand. (NIV)

Because he has done so much for me I want to shout this from the rooftops: there is life beyond brokenness! Jesus can heal our broken hearts and give us a new lease on life! It is my prayer that these stories will inspire you to give thanks to our loving Father for the transforming power of Jesus to create beauty out of our brokenness. And if he heals your broken heart, you must tell others the good news. Many hurting people need to know! His gracious plan is that the redeemed will offer hope to the brokenhearted!

Walter Albritton, sjc
Servant of Jesus Christ

The Cabin
Wetumpka, Alabama
October, 2014

Table of Contents

1

Brokenness will not have the last word!

Many friends offered congratulations when I turned 82. One asked me what great lessons I had learned about life. I smiled but declined to answer, feeling I had nothing profound to share.

After pondering the question one great lesson came to mind. That lesson has to do with the brokenness and pain that comes eventually to everyone. Each of us must find a way to handle a broken heart. How we deal with it determines whether we shall live well or poorly.

While brokenness does color my life, I can choose the color. That is the great lesson. I have a choice about how I shall react. I can refuse to allow hardship to paint my life black, the color of gloom and despair. I can work my way through tears and heartache and choose blue or yellow, red or green, colors of hope and joy.

I love the Gloria and Bill Gaither song, "Something Beautiful." It offers profound truth in very few words:

> *Something beautiful, something good;*
> *all my confusion he understood;*
> *all I had to offer him was brokenness and strife,*
> *but he made something beautiful of my life.*

Everything depends on how I respond to the failure, pain or brokenness of my life. If I choose to pity myself I allow my hardship to defeat me. Hardship can ruin me if I choose the route of cynicism or stoicism.

The key to victory lies in my understanding of God. It matters greatly what I believe about God's attitude toward me. I am on the road to victory if I believe that God cares about my plight, that he "understands." This is a matter of faith; I can choose to believe that God cares for me even though my hardship may be the result of my own poor decisions.

Every pastor visits nursing homes to offer love and hope to lonely old people. Early on I realized I could communicate the faith more effectively by singing it than preaching it. So I cannot count the times I have sung these words in a nursing home:

> *No one understand like Jesus,*
> *He's a friend beyond compare;*
> *Meet Him at the throne of mercy,*
> *He is waiting for you there.*
> *No one understands like Jesus.*
> *When the days are dark and grim;*
> *No one is so near, so dear as Jesus*
> *Cast your every care on Him.*

Songs like that one by John W. Peterson convey a comforting, eternal truth – that God understands our suffering. Believing that, we can turn to Jesus, the living Christ, for comfort, hope and healing.

Another key to recovery involves the word "offer." I can sit in the ashes of my brokenness and whine or I can "offer" my hardship to God in the hope that he can create beauty out of the mess I have made. It cheers me to remember that many people have overcome their brokenness by "offering" it to God, letting him take over. A friend, grieving over the death of her husband, seemed unable to move beyond her sorrow. Then one day she walked up to me smiling. She was different. Sadness no longer controlled her. "What happened?" I asked. She replied simply, "I gave my sorrow to Jesus; I don't have it anymore. I am free!"

Another wonderful gospel hymn (also a good one to sing in nursing homes) illustrates how this can happen. It is "Tell It to Jesus" by Jeremiah E. Rankin:

Are you weary, are you heavy-hearted?
Tell it to Jesus, Tell it to Jesus;
Are you grieving over joys departed?
Tell it to Jesus alone.
Tell it to Jesus, Tell it to Jesus,
He is a friend that's well-known;
You've no other such a friend or brother,
Tell it to Jesus alone.

When Jesus is Lord we can "tell" him about our heartaches and expect him not only to understand but to touch our lives with healing love.

Fanny Crosby and George Matheson are good examples to follow in facing our brokenness. Both were blind but refused to complain. Each offered their blindness to God and received the strength to compose beautiful songs which millions enjoy singing. They refused to let their brokenness "blind" them to their opportunity to live useful lives. The singer Steven Curtis Chapman once wrote about a dry spell in his life when he was desperate for a breakthrough in his spirit. Wanting God to do something, just to show up, he went out in the woods to pray. There he stacked some rocks to symbolize an altar and began to pray. As he was praying, he began to smell cedar. It was so strong that it distracted him from praying.

He opened his eyes and began looking around. Soon he saw a little cedar tree which he had snapped in half by stepping on it. The smell was coming from that small, broken tree. Chapman saw it as a sign of God's coming to him. He wrote down these words, "The fragrance of the broken."

God does provide a "fragrance" which we may learn to cherish as we deal with our own brokenness and that of our loved ones. Like the little cedar tree, it may not be obvious. We have to look for it as Chapman did. Finding it, we begin to enjoy the "aroma of grace."

My friend "Miss Jimmy" was a poet who became blind as an adult. She also declined to complain. She even chose to believe that her blindness was a blessing. It helped her to discover blessings she would not have known had her sight not failed.

"I had not bothered to read the Bible very much," she said, "but when I became blind, I began to listen to the Bible on cassette tapes. Only then did I understand why it is considered the greatest book ever written. Listening to God's Word in my blindness has helped me see the light."

Brokenness and pain comes soon or late to us all. Whining about it or asking "Why me?" only increases our misery. As we face the pain with honesty and hope, something wonderful can occur. Character can happen. We can become finer people because we have faced our troubles with courage. We can become better instead of bitter.

Courage is contagious. Deal with your brokenness bravely, with a positive spirit, and your example will encourage someone else. The challenge is to find a way to smell the "aroma of grace" in our pain and allow the fragrance of our brokenness to sweeten the atmosphere of our lives. While pain is inevitable, misery is optional.

The great lesson I have learned about handling hardship is this: God understands my pain and is willing to help me refuse to let brokenness have the last word. He has a great track record for making something beautiful out of brokenness. +

2

You can still hear the laughter after they're gone

Somewhere my wife found a plaque with these words on it: "If you love somebody enough, you can still hear the laughter after they're gone." The plaque sits on a dresser in our bedroom. In front of it is a picture of my sister Laurida and another of our son David. Each one was laughing heartily when the picture was made.

The author of that statement was right. When I look at the picture of my sister I can still hear her boisterous laughter though she died 20 years ago. Never timid, Laurida laughed "all over" when she laughed. Watching her laugh was more enjoyable than whatever we were laughing about.

She must have been a wonderful mother because her seven children are all fine people. Like my mother Laurida was a dedicated "homemaker." Her great love was her family and her children knew it – and were blessed by it. I am sure each one was shaped in some way by the influence of a godly mother who left this world all too soon. I don't remember seeing my sister cry but one time. That time she shed tears of joy while lying in bed, soon to succumb to cancer. The occasion was the marriage of her daughter Margie to Warren Clark Johnson. I joined them in holy matrimony at the foot of her bed because Laurida was too weak to have made a trip to church.

I remember Laurida laughing every time we were together. She loved life and when she laughed she put her whole body into it. So it's true – I loved her enough that I can look at her picture and still hear her laughing.

Memories of our son David are a bit different. I remember him crying many times, especially during the long months of his terminal illness. Pain produces tears – especially for children. And their pain is compounded for parents who are helpless to explain why an innocent child must suffer.

One of my worst memories is of David begging me to not let a nurse hurt him with needles while giving him a blood transfusion. I could think of no way to explain why his daddy would allow someone to hurt him. The nurse insisted that I hold him still while she inserted the needle in his arm. On many days he cried himself to sleep in my arms or his mother's arms.

But we made no pictures of David crying. We did make several of him laughing vigorously. He did have moments of sheer joy. Those are the pictures we cherish. One of the best of those pictures sits in a small frame in front of the plaque. When my wife put it there it was her way of affirming the words: "If you love somebody enough, you can still hear the laughter after they're gone."

Life is a mixture of tears and laughs, of joy and sorrow, of pain and pleasure. Were there no pain we could not appreciate the pleasure. The challenge is to not let pain and sorrow defeat us. Faith in a loving God who hurts when his children hurt is the key to winning.

Sometimes when I stop and listen to the laughter of Laurida and David, I think I hear the Father laughing also. His victorious laughter mingled with theirs reminds me that the dark night of sorrow must inevitably give way to the joy of the eternal morning. Joy can laugh at sorrow for joy will have the last word.

Am I sure of that? Yes, I am. It was confirmed in my heart by the One who said he came that we might have joy. Laughter springs from that joy in our hearts. +

3

What I learned in a Virginia hospital

I have never agreed with the idea that "God put me flat on my back so I would have to look up." God would have to be capricious to do that and the God I find in the Bible does not act impulsively as human beings do.

God does allow bad things to happen to people. But he does not arrange trouble for people to get their attention. It does happen that in the midst of calamity God often gets our attention. Many of us do "look up" or reach out to God when trouble gets the best of us. So in that sense misfortune can be a good thing; it can remind us that we need God.

Much of our suffering is the result of willfully disobeying God. He tells us how to live and we choose to live like we please. Disobedience leads to misery and we find ourselves flat on our back with no place to look but up.

I love the Book of Jeremiah for this very reason. The weeping prophet tells his people, the Israelites, that their suffering is the consequence of their sin. They had broken the covenant God made with them. So, the prophet declares, God's justice will be served. The people will be punished. Sadness will be their food night and day.

But that is not the end of the story! There is hope for your future, Jeremiah tells the people, because God in his mercy is going to bring the exiles back to Jerusalem. The Holy City will be restored.

When God does this, Jeremiah says, he will make a new covenant with his people, bringing together the northern and southern kingdoms and making them one again. The new covenant will not be a covenant of laws and rituals; it will be a covenant of the heart.

The new covenant will demonstrate God's great mercy. He will forgive the sins of his rebellious children and he *"will remember their sin no more."* When you read that, does it sink in? That is a staggering thought – the God we have offended will *forget* our sins! Highlight that in your Bible! Never forget it! God loves us so much that he will not only forgive us; he will forget about our sin! He will wipe the slate clean! Glory! What a promise!

When I reflect on what Jeremiah said, I feel like falling to my knees. This was a magnificent moment in history! God gave Jeremiah a glimpse of the future, allowing him to see that day when the blood of Jesus would become the only blood that need be shed for the forgiveness of sins!

Can you remember a time when you saw little hope for your future? A time when you were caught in the web of your own sinfulness and wondered if God really cared about you?

I can remember such a time in my own life. I had pushed myself relentlessly, trying to do ministry in my own strength. I had relied on my own ingenuity. I had neglected my family to further my own selfish ambitions. Then, flat on my back in a Virginia hospital, I was told I that I had almost died from a bleeding ulcer. Weeping and helpless, flat on my back, I looked up to God for help. In my own eyes my future was cloudy and uncertain.

During that time I turned tearfully to the Bible, pleading with God for help. He led me to read the 31st chapter of Jeremiah, one of the most powerful passages in the Bible. I can still remember how deeply God stirred my soul as I read:

"Restrain your voice from weeping and your eyes from tears, for your work will be rewarded," declares the Lord. *"They will return from the land of the enemy. So there is hope for your future,"* declares the Lord. *"Your children will return to their own land."* (Verses 16 & 17, NIV)

What God told Jeremiah long ago, he told me that morning! My despair was lifted! Hope came into my heart like a rushing wind! I was soon made well and able to resume my ministry.

What is more, during all the years since that divine moment, God has continued to keep His promises to me – not because of my worthiness but because he is faithful. My gratitude for his mercy remains the constant cry of my heart.

In that hospital in Fairfax, Virginia, flat on my back, I looked up and learned from a loving, forgiving God that there was hope for my future. And that hope, I believe with all my heart, is available still to all who will look up and call upon His Name! +

4

The incredible power of forgiveness

Forgiveness is power. It may be the most positive power in the world. Forgiveness can break chains that hold us in bondage to the past. It can set us free to have peace in the present and hope for the future.

A family cannot be healthy without the constant practice of forgiveness. That is because no one is perfect and sooner or later each of us will need forgiveness for having said or done something stupid. I know because I am chairman of the Stupid Comments Club.

Soon after my wife and I were married my mother gave us a framed copy of this profound statement: "Marriage: May there be such a oneness between you that when one weeps the other will taste salt." It has hung in every bedroom we have shared during all the years of our marriage.

We have shed a lot of tears. We have tasted a lot of salt. Again and again it has been forgiveness that saved and restored our marriage. That philosophy must have helped Mama and Daddy stay married too; they had checked off 67 years when Daddy died.

A wounded relationship with my wife is at the top of my pain list. When our oneness is fractured I am absolutely miserable. I cannot focus on the task at hand. All I can think about is "How can I fix this and get delivered from this terrible pain?"

Early in our marriage we sometimes endured a two-weeks "mad." Rather than say "I am sorry," we stubbornly breathed the air of righteous indignation. Anger and disappointment drove us to punish each other by withholding forgiveness. We were young and foolishly we must have thought we would "live forever."

Fortunately we got better at "making up." Now that we are old we can recover from a breakup quickly, sometimes within minutes. Actually we seldom have a spat these days; neither of us has the energy for a good fight. Perhaps that is one of the blessings of old age.

"Making up" is really one of the sweetest experiences of life. The process is not complicated. You come down off your high horse and admit you were wrong. You ask forgiveness. You offer forgiveness. You accept forgiveness. The result is magnificent. You exchange misery for joy – and the joy of oneness releases an extraordinary peace within your soul. Life is suddenly beautiful again.

When you become weary of pouting and chaffing because your feelings have been hurt, you might try saying "I was wrong; please forgive me. I want to put this behind us."

Forgiveness is powerful. Offer it and pretty soon you may be tasting salt. And when you are miserable nothing tastes better than the salt of oneness restored. +

5

Inviting the brokenhearted to taste and see

They buried their precious daughter last week. Cora was only eleven. You might suppose they were still in tears, struggling under the weight of their sorrow.

But not Darlene and Arthur. Instead Darlene was posting on Facebook a powerful witness about the goodness of God. I loved the way she used a piece of bread to get our attention.

A friend invited Darlene to taste a piece of cranberry-walnut bread. She liked it so much she bought a loaf. Then she invited another friend to taste the delicious bread. The friend liked it too.

Darlene says that is how we should share the Lord with other people. Tell people about God's goodness and invite them to try Him for themselves. This, she says, is what David recommends in Psalm 34:8 – "Taste and see that the Lord is good."

Then Darlene drives home her big idea – that God is good even when death robs you of a beloved child. You might think the two-year trial of Cora's struggle with a brain tumor would have driven these parents away from God. But Darlene says, "This trial has not turned us from God but has drawn us closer to Him." She insists that they are more keenly aware of God's love now than ever before.

What a testimony from grieving parents! That same Psalm 34 has another great verse in it, a verse that explains the strong faith held by Darlene and Arthur. These are the words of verse 18: "The Lord is close to the brokenhearted and saves those who are crushed in spirit." Yes, that describes our God!

The Bible convinces me that God hears the cries of his children. Go back to the days of Jeremiah, for example, and you find such a God. Jerusalem had been destroyed. Most of the people were exiles and slaves in a foreign land. But some were allowed to remain in Jerusalem where Jeremiah helped them understand God's love for the brokenhearted.

Overwhelmed by sorrow, uprooted from their homeland, the Israelites had little hope for the future. They had disobeyed God. Now they were enduring God's punishment for their sins.

But in the midst of their affliction, God came. Despite their stubbornness, God did not abandon them. God never stopped loving them. In fact, just when they needed it the most, God gave them the precious gift of hope, a gift "made flesh" in a man, the prophet Jeremiah.

Jeremiah saw beyond the present suffering; he saw a future full of the goodness of God. The prophet saw that hope is greater than grief, that joy is greater than sorrow. Few greater visions of God are found in Holy Scripture than this one by the weeping prophet:

"Because of the Lord's great love we are not consumed, for his compassions never fail. They are new every morning; great is your faithfulness." (Lamentations 3:22-23, NIV)

This vision birthed the beloved hymn, "Great is Thy Faithfulness." The song often brings me to my knees in worship, especially the words, "All I have needed, Thy Hand hath provided." I want to cry out "Yes, Lord, Yes!"

What a great truth for us to embrace and live by: God's mercies are new every morning! No matter what pain we endured in the night, God's mercies are as sure as the morning light and ours for the asking. Morning suggests breakfast. When we rise from a night's rest we feel fresh; we have fresh energy. The aroma of fresh coffee makes us glad to be alive.

Fresh bread smells good and tastes delicious. Think of our disappointment if all we had for breakfast was day-old coffee and stale bread! No so God's mercies; they are fresh every morning!

But not only do we have bread – like Darlene's delicious cranberry-walnut bread. We have the Bread of Heaven whose name is Jesus! And like Darlene we can invite those who are brokenhearted to "Taste and see that the Lord is good."

Our thanks to Darlene and Arthur for reminding us, in the midst

13

of their own sorrow, that God is good. He is faithful. He keeps his promise to comfort the brokenhearted. Our troubles may weigh us down but we need not stay down. We can turn to the God whose eye is on the sparrow and know that he cares about our sorrows. He hurts when we hurt. And every new morning can be a new beginning because His compassion never fails! Yes! +

6

The lonely road of sorrow

Grief is one of the common threads of life. It links us all together. Since every person will die the painful loss of loved ones is inevitable. And loss causes pain and struggle.

Loss, however, does not have to be endured alone. Support is available. Though our society has spawned a "culture of violence," that is not the whole story. There are churches, counselors and agencies that are ready to help us walk the lonely road of sorrow. And each of us can offer love and encouragement to the hurting persons in our circles of friends.

This is one of the beautiful aspects of being a human being. Each of us has the capacity to share one another's burdens, to offer a shoulder to cry on, to simply "be there" for someone whose pain seems unbearable. You can fake love but you cannot fake being there. And being there with a hurting friend can make a difference.

Grief feels like the bottom has fallen out of your world. Someone you loved is missing. A chair is empty. Tools once used are now idle. You feel numb and helpless. Yet life goes on. And you must find a way to go on with your own life.

We must find the strength to deal with the reality of death. Little help comes from reading a poem that says, "I did not die; I am still here with you." No, the person who died in our arms and was buried last week is actually dead and gone.

I once visited an old man who belonged to my church. He was about 80 and lived alone. While we chatted he told me about his beloved wife who had died about 20 years previously. "Would you like to see her room?" he asked. I was puzzled but said yes so we walked down the hall.

Opening the door to a bedroom, he said, "Everything is still just like it was the day she died," he said. I was stunned by what I saw: an unmade bed with a dress on the footboard, a hair brush and lipstick lying on a dresser with one drawer partially opened, and the entire scene covered with cobwebs. It was something you would expect to see only in a horror movie.

I prayed with the old man and departed sorrowfully for I knew I had met a man whose family and friends had failed him. Yes, he had failed himself. But that is why we are in this world – to help a brother or a sister find a helpful way to handle grief. And the truth is, some need more help than others.

Take a look around you. You will likely find someone who is struggling with the emotions that grief produces: anger, guilt, bitterness, emptiness, fear and self-pity. You may be able to help that person not by urging them to "get over it and move on" but by simply walking beside them until the pain diminishes.

If nothing else you might remind your hurting friend that God hurts too, just like his children hurt, when someone dies. He is that kind of God, a God who cares and is ready to help us when we are mourning the loss of a loved one. And he wants his children to help one another as they walk the painful and lonely journey called grief.
The privilege of providing loving support and encouragement to a fellow human being may be the secret of a life well lived. And sooner or later each of us will need that support. +

7

Simplicity – doorway to joy

Students of the Bible are inspired by the example of Daniel. He was an Old Testament prophet with steel in his backbone. Despite King Darius' threat of death to the disobedient, Daniel ignored the king's law to stop praying to his God. He continued to pray openly and on his knees, three times a day. The penalty for breaking this law was death (thrown to the lions).

Officials of the king, jealous of Daniel's popularity with the king, had deceived the king into passing an ordinance forbidding anyone to pray to any god other than King Darius. The naïve king did not realize that the law was designed to eliminate Daniel. Caught praying, Daniel was hauled before the king and thrown to the lions.

The next morning the king found that Daniel was alive. God had closed the mouths of the lions. Darius was "exceedingly glad" and decreed that all the people of Persia "should tremble and fear before the God of Daniel: For he is the living God, enduring forever." Daniel's trust in God was so strong that he did not panic in the face of death.

Centuries later the Apostle Paul demonstrated the same confidence in God. He kept the faith despite persecution and threats of death. Both Daniel and Paul were disciplined in prayer. Their confidence sprang from daily communion with God. Their examples inspire us to pray.

There are special people whose examples motivate each of us to seek a more disciplined spiritual life. God used both the writing and the example of Richard J. Foster to inspire me to take more seriously the holy habits of the spiritual life.

I met Foster before his books made him the best known Quaker in the world. When I arrived in Wichita, Kansas, to speak to the student body at Friends University, Foster met me at the airport. Then a professor of theology at the university, he had volunteered to serve as my host for the week. We loaded my luggage into his rundown station wagon and headed to the campus.

His casual dress, and his warm and unassuming manner, made me feel welcome and comfortable. His gracious hospitality made me feel at home in a strange town. I shared how much I had enjoyed his book, *Celebration of Discipline*. Neither of us had any idea then that his book would sell more than a million copies and be named one of the top ten books of the 20th Century.

I realized later that a beautiful thing had happened to me. Foster made no effort to impress me. He put aside his own work and took time to be my host. Months later it dawned on me that Richard Foster, the most famous man ever to serve as my chauffeur, was simply practicing the simplicity that he describes in his books as one of the basic spiritual disciplines of devout Christians. His book, *Freedom of Simplicity*, is an excellent read. And I know from personal experience the man practices what he preaches!

When I read Foster's *Celebration of Discipline* from time to time, I guard against heaping shame upon myself for lack of discipline. Shame seldom motivates us to grow. Guilt hinders our spiritual progress if we allow it to hang around. But guilt can help us if we allow it to motivate us to forgive ourselves for past failures and make a fresh start in living a more disciplined life.

The best way to approach spiritual disciplines is to set aside some time and get into them one day at a time. We should make sure we have the right motive – not to become more pious but more useful servants. The greatest reward of spiritual growth is a deeper friendship with God. And that friendship is deepened by our service to others.
I know a man who runs a hundred miles a week. He wants to become stronger so he can compete well in his next marathon. If he can be disciplined in order to run well, surely I can practice holy habits in order to become a more effective servant of Christ.

Where shall we begin? Each of us must decide. As for me, I feel the Spirit nudging me to become more disciplined in prayer and to live a more simple life. Simplicity is the doorway to true joy. Freedom from the tyranny of things will bless me – and make me a blessing.

Begin anywhere the Spirit leads you. Don't wait for someone to join you. Be a self-starter. Be disciplined regardless of what others may think. Be a Daniel. The time to get started is now. +

8

Do your best and leave the rest to God

Weeping for others is as old as the human race. The prophet Jeremiah wept for his people and cried out for the Balm of Gilead:

"My grief is beyond healing; my heart is broken. Listen to the weeping of my people; it can be heard all across the land. 'Has the LORD abandoned Jerusalem?' the people ask. 'Is her King no longer there?' 'Oh, why have they angered me with their carved idols and worthless gods?' asks the LORD. 'The harvest is finished, and the summer is gone,' the people cry, 'yet we are not saved!' I weep for the hurt of my people. I am stunned and silent, mute with grief. Is there no medicine in Gilead? Is there no physician there? Why is there no healing for the wounds of my people?" (Jeremiah 8:18-22, NLT).

Jesus has such compassion for the sick that he healed many of them. On one occasion he showed remarkable kindness to a deaf man who could not speak:

A deaf man with a speech impediment was brought to him, and the people begged Jesus to lay his hands on the man to heal him. Jesus led him away from the crowd so they could be alone. He put his fingers into the man's ears. Then, spitting onto his own fingers, he touched the man's tongue with the spittle. Looking up to heaven, he sighed and said, "Ephphatha," which means, "Be opened!" Instantly the man could hear perfectly and his tongue was freed so he could speak plainly! Jesus told the crowd not to tell anyone, but the more he told them not to, the more they spread the news. They were completely amazed and said again and again, "Everything he does is wonderful. He even makes the deaf to hear and gives speech to those who cannot speak" (Mark 7:32-37, NLT).

Not wanting to embarrass the man, Jesus took him aside from the crowd to minister to him. What beautiful compassion! He did not want the poor man to feel humiliated before curious onlookers. In much the same way doctors and nurses take the sick aside to help them in privacy. As they work with patients, they get to know them; they become friends. But some of them do not get well; they suffer and die. Caregivers suffer too because it hurts to see others suffer.

What are we to do with the feelings that overwhelm us when our family and friends are suffering? We have at least two options:

1) We can stifle our compassion, become stoic and refuse to get emotionally involved. By refusing to care deeply we can protect ourselves from suffering. We can say that life, like war, is hell and that is simply the way things are. We can grit our teeth and refuse to love so we won't be hurt. Some people choose this way to deal with pain.

2) Thankfully there is a better option. We can seize the moment and care deeply for hurting people and help them make the most of every day until life is over. While Jesus could do more than we can do, we can make a difference. We have something to offer the sick that is more important than medicine.

Solomon expressed it well when he said, *"A cheerful heart is good medicine, but a crushed spirit dries up the bones"* (Proverbs 17:22, NIV). A cheerful spirit can make a powerful difference to the sick and dying. God prescribes it even when doctors do not.

Since we cannot prevent either suffering or death, we must not slack from doing what we can. We can be at peace and compassionately do the best we can and leave the rest to God. He is in charge of life and death. It is not within our power to keep people alive indefinitely. Death is a natural part of life and there are mysteries too complex for our limited minds to understand on this side. In doing our best we may learn some valuable lessons. These are a few I have learned:

1. Suffering is a great teacher. It teaches us to value every waking moment. I was brash, cocky and carefree until our son David was diagnosed with leukemia. Then my real education began. I realized

what pain doctors and nurses endure in order to serve others. Dr. T. Fort Bridges and his staff in Nashville were gracious, loving people; they hurt with us during David's 9-month battle with leukemia. Our crash course in suffering culminated one morning when Dr. Nels Ferre took us in his arms and said, "God hurts like you hurt." We have never forgotten the compassion of this good man who lifted the dead body of our son off the bed and asked the Lord to receive his soul.

2. We are not alone. God is with us. His name is Emmanuel, God with us! My wife almost died from a terrible lung disease. One day suddenly she was better. The doctor did not know why. My wife complained that it was terribly hot and stuffy in her hospital room. Then she felt a cool breeze in the room. She said, "I felt a Presence. I looked around but could see no one. But I felt someone was in the room. Then, all of a sudden, I felt well." The doctor confirmed her wellness the next morning and dismissed her. He had no explanation for her recovery.

We are not alone as we walk the halls of a hospital. There will be times when Christ will seem so present that you can feel his hand on your shoulder. When you are weak, He will give you the strength to carry on and you will know then that He is with you. He helps popes and preachers but He also helps caring people share his compassion with the sick.

3. Gentleness and kindness are more valuable than diamonds, especially when you are suffering. When I almost died because of a blood clot I remembered Paul's words: "The time of my departure is at hand." I thought my time was up. But the doctors and nurses who cared for me gave me hope and treated me with unbelievable kindness, far beyond the requirements of professional care.

As you care for a suffering friend or relative do the best you can and leave the rest to God. Offer every ounce of kindness and cheer you possess and depend on Christ to refill the reservoir within you. The more compassion you give away, the more He will restore your supply.

He will help you to grow in your capacity to love people – even those you can love only for a little while. As you feel pain, and shed tears, remember that Jesus was acquainted with grief. Offer your tears to him and allow him to turn your tears into the wine of joy. Never look for a way to avoid being hurt by the suffering of others. Remember you are made in the image of the God who hurts like you hurt. Pain is part of his plan for shaping us into the compassionate servants he wants us to become.

James reminds us that our life is but a shadow, like a vapor that appears for a little while and then vanishes. While we have life, let us do the very best we can with it and leave the rest to God. +

9

The falling of a giant oak

My friend Ted Cheek was not a perfect man. There are no perfect men among us. Since time began there has been only one and his name was Jesus.

We all have our flaws. Ted had his. I have mine. You have yours. Of our weaknesses we are all aware. That is why we long for our friends to love us "warts and all." And that is really the only way people can be loved. Love finds a way to leap over a person's faults.

What inspires us all is to see a fellow human being rise above his flaws and make a difference with his life. Ted Cheek was such a man.

In his early years Ted's problems seemed to overpower him. More than once he was on the verge of defeat. But Ted was a fighter. He kept clawing and scratching for a way to win. And he did.

The difference for Ted was faith. Like most of us Ted struggled with many issues. But finally he found his way out of the woods by becoming a devout Christian. He became a new man in the best sense of that phrase so common in Christian parlance.

A changed man, Ted never took credit for the change. He would tell you emphatically, "The Lord did it; he took all my problems off my back." And those who knew Ted best realized that the Lord had begun changing Ted's question marks into exclamation points. Ted had discarded his doubts and embraced faith in God wholeheartedly.

The transformation of Ted's life led him to become more than a church member and more than a church "leader." His faith rubbed off on those around him and as the years rolled on he helped his church to grow even as his own faith was growing.

One of the Old Testament prophets used an interesting phase to describe people whose lives God had changed. Isaiah said, "They will be called oaks of righteousness, a planting of the Lord for the display of his splendor" (61:3, NIV).

In the forest an oak can be quite a tree. A giant oak is impressive. Ted was a big man physically but even more he was a giant oak of the faith. Though not perfect Ted was an "oak of righteousness," a man sold out to the God who had rescued him from his weaknesses.

Ted's final battle was a gallant struggle with ALS (Amyotrophic lateral sclerosis), commonly known as Lou Gehrig's disease. His faith was tested but it did not fail.

During a year of struggle and suffering Ted looked death in the face and refused to be intimidated. His faith grew stronger. He prayed. He sang. He witnessed. He testified to the love of the God he had trusted with his whole being. He immersed himself in the Holy Scriptures. When you visited Ted and Ellen you realized that God was all over that house. Their home was a house of faith where Jesus was loved and served.

Ted did not go whimpering to the grave. He knew the death of his body would usher him into the nearer presence of his God. He showed his family and friends how to die – with absolute confidence that Jesus had prepared a place for him in heaven, a room in the Father's House. Ted loved to sing and though he could barely hear he delighted to have his friends come to his home and sing together his favorite songs of faith. All his life Ted loved the songs of Johnny Cash. As a fitting footnote to Ted's uniqueness, a medley of Cash's songs were played by his friend Guy Johnson as Ted's body was taken out of the church following the funeral celebration of his life.

Ted enjoyed Josh Turner's song, "Long Black Train." The song begins with the words, "There's a long black train comin' down the line, feeding off the souls that are lost and cryin'." There is a warning in the song to "watch out brother" because the "devil's drivin' that long black train."

I think Ted liked that quaint song because of this affirmation in the lyrics: "You know there's victory in the Lord, I say Victory in the Lord; cling to the Father and His Holy name and don't go ridin' on that long black train."

25

The devil had to be disappointed because he never succeeded in getting Ted to get on board that long black train. Instead Ted boarded that "sweet chariot" that came down one day and gave him a ride to the Father's House.

Ted Cheek – a good friend who was indeed a giant oak that the good Lord planted in our midst to display his splendor. +

10

Songs remind us of people we know

Some songs are connected, in my mind, to particular persons. When I hear "Clair de Lune" by Claude Debussy, for example, I think about my wife. Dean dearly loves that mesmerizing music.

George Beverly Shea comes to mind when I hear "How Great Thou Art." He must have sung that song a thousand times in Billy Graham crusades.

"I Saw the Light" reminds me of Hank Williams who wrote the song. I wonder if he really did "trade the wrong for the right" before he passed away one night in his Cadillac. I hope so.

"Wade in the Water" reminds me of Eddie Smith and his quartet. Thirty years ago Eddie, Greg, Tommy and Bill taught me to love that stirring spiritual. I loved to listen to them sing about our Lord.

"Man of Sorrows," a hymn, brings Joni Eareckson Tada to mind. I was not familiar with this song until I heard Joni sing it in a testimony. You may recall that Joni, though a paraplegic, is a well-known artist, author and speaker. She broke her neck diving into a pool during her late teens.

In her testimony Joni tells how, before her accident, she played on the school hockey team with her best friend Jackie. After losing a close game one night they began crying while riding the bus home. They remembered that they were Christians so they started singing, "Man of Sorrows, what a name, for the Son of God who came, ruined sinners to reclaim. Hallelujah, what a Savior."

Sometime later, now crippled, Joni was surprised one night to have her friend Jackie slip into the hospital after hours and crawl into the hospital bed beside her. Jackie held Joni's paralyzed hand up in the air and began to sing, "Man of Sorrows...."

Joni said that her faith in the goodness of God was restored that night as once again she and Jackie sang that hymn together. She began to believe again that God is good even if you are imprisoned in a wheelchair.

But that is not the end of the story. Years later Joni heard that tragedy had befallen her friend Jackie. She and her husband had separated; their son Joshua was dead. A troubled teenager, Joshua became addicted to drugs. One night he left a suicide note in the mailbox on the street, set himself on fire and burned his dad's house down around him.

Joni went to Jackie, embraced her and once again they sang together the stirring hymn, "Man of Sorrows." Eventually Jackie found peace, and said to Joni, "I've got this cross around my neck. It's the one my son gave me. Every time I start to feel desperate, like I can't make it, like I'm in prison, then I hold on to this cross until I have peace." I can never sing "Man of Sorrows" without thinking about Joni and Jackie and how that hymn helped them face their hardships.

I will mention one final song – "I Stand Amazed in the Presence of Jesus the Nazarene." It reminds me of myself. I do love that song! It stirs my heart like few others. When your heart is broken the strengthening presence of Jesus can change everything.

Songs make such a powerful difference in our lives. I hope you have a favorite that can be a channel of blessing to you now and then. +

11

Enough grace to get us through tough times

Sometimes I hear a Christian say rather glibly, "No matter what you have to face, God's grace is sufficient." Though I believe that is true I know there have been times in my own life when I was not sure. When truly bad things happen to good people, even the best of us will wonder if God's grace will be enough to get us through the heartache and pain.

So I thank God the Second Letter of Paul to the Corinthians is included in the Bible. It is a short letter that contains a powerful message. Without that word from the Lord every persecuted Christian might be tempted to wallow in self-pity. Fortunately we can read Paul's description of the troubles he faced as a servant of Christ. Upon reading that most of us will admit that God allowed Paul to suffer far more than we have suffered.

Years ago a friend stunned me with these words, "The people who have hurt me the most have been my friends within the church." I was shocked because I knew the man to be a devout Christian. Over the years I have lived into an understanding of his sad comment.

I too have been hurt deeply by the sharp tongues of fellow Christians. But I have also hurt Christian friends with my own tongue. And while I am quick to excuse myself I recognize that my "suffering" is hardly worth mentioning when compared to that of the Apostle Paul. Every time I read again what Paul endured I hear the Inner Voice asking, "How dare you complain? You should be ashamed of yourself." And usually I am ashamed.

But back the question: Is the grace of God always enough to get us through the troubles we face? I can give only one answer: Yes, yes, yes – God's grace is sufficient no matter how harsh our troubles! Even when doubt comes knocking on my heart's door I have to say, "Trouble, you are not greater than my God. And his grace is sufficient for every need I face!"

The amazing thing is that God's power can be made "perfect" in our weakness. And the power of Christ is just as available to us as it was to Paul. That being true, we too can handle insults, hardships, persecution and trouble in such a way that Christ receives glory and honor. The question is: are we willing to trust God to the point that his all-sufficient grace becomes transparent, or active, in our daily lives?

Paul shames me when he declares that he had decided to "boast" of the things that showcased his weaknesses. He even admitted that once he had been "a basket case," having to run for his life when his friends lowered him in a basket from a window in the wall in Damascus.

How many of us are mature enough to boast of our weaknesses? I find it hard to do. We are sons and daughters of a culture that teaches us to value impressive "credentials" and counterfeit "honors." Paul had lost any confidence in his own achievements; the only thing he valued now was his relationship to Jesus Christ. Knowing Christ and serving him was all that mattered.

As we mature in faith we gain a new perspective about what really matters. Our desires and our values change. We cherish our acceptance by God and no longer thirst for "the applause of men." I was proud one day to be included in a list of *Who's Who in American Colleges and Universities*. I bought the book so my friends could see how important I was. Years later I realized how foolish I had been to value such a thing and threw the book in the trash bin. Though we may not become perfect in this life at least we can outgrow some of our foolishness.

Suffering is evidently God's plan for our lives. He allows and uses suffering to make us better people and more useful servants of others. Like Paul we may know the pain of having a "thorn in the flesh" that for some reason God will not remove.

Why does God not answer our prayers to deliver us from our thorns in the flesh? I have no answer other than this: He does answer our prayers; sometimes He says no or not now. And for reasons that may not become clear to us this side of heaven.

The great lesson Paul teaches us is this: He learned to depend not on himself but on the grace of God. Here is one of the great secrets of the Christian life. The Christian life demands a vital union with Christ. Life works God's way when we live in Christ and welcome his living in us. Shipwreck without rescue is the ultimate end of those who trust in their own strength instead of the grace of God.

Pride leads us to trust in our own cleverness rather than admit our weakness and our need of God's grace. But when we realize the futility of showcasing our own strength we can admit our weaknesses and turn in simple faith to Christ. When we do he is willing to let his power dwell in us and give us victory in the midst of our troubles.

Then, and only then, can we celebrate the eternal truth affirmed by Paul that no matter what we must face, God's grace is always sufficient! +

12

A lesson that took forty years to learn

In my fortieth year I learned a very important lesson about being a father. By that time my wife had given birth to five sons. Our first son had died at three but his brothers were then 15, 12, 10 and 8.

We were learning how to be a family. The oldest son had quickly taught us that raising teenagers was more of a challenge than we had anticipated. As teenage boys will do he was testing our authority daily and pushing hard against whatever boundaries we had set.

Our boundaries were mostly reactionary, not well thought out. When the boys got in trouble we responded by establishing a rule. We were writing our book of rules on the run. I learned by trial and error that children need boundaries.

In the meantime my focus was almost entirely on my work. My career as a minister was my primary concern. I worked hard at what I was doing, the result of the work ethic instilled in me by my hardworking father. He worked from daylight till dark as a farmer. I did the same as a preacher.

At the time I was traveling a lot because I was "in demand." Many months I was out of town more than half the time. I left the needs of the family up to my wife. Sometimes she would punch me in the stomach with a comment like this: "Tell your father goodbye, children; he is off to save the world again." And I knew she was thinking "while his family goes to hell."

My wife would shame me occasionally into taking time off for "time with the family." But even on a family picnic or a trip to the park my mind was often on what mattered most to me – my work. As a result our family outings led not to harmony but disharmony.

As the tension mounted I realized that my wife was not a happy camper. She told me bluntly one day as I was about to catch another plane, "I am sick and tired of being the father and the mother of this family." I left that day as I left many other days – sick and troubled inside. Things were going badly for us and I knew it.

So it was that in the year I turned forty I found myself alone in a retreat center in Indiana. I had come to a crossroads. My wife was miserable and our family was scrambled eggs. What was worse, I did not have a clue how to fix the problem.

Deeply troubled I prayed hard, desperately seeking guidance from the Lord. And it was the Lord who reminded me of a question a man had asked me a few days before: "If you could do anything you wanted to do, what would you do?" Pondering that question, which shook me to the core, I found the answer to my dilemma.

My heart pounding, I realized that more than anything else in the world I wanted to be a successful father and husband. My career would be like sand in my hands if I lost the love and respect of my boys and my wife. I admitted to myself that my wife was right and I was wrong. There, in those hours alone with God, I made the decision to put my family first, ahead of my career.

I came home, gave up my traveling ministry and asked my bishop to appoint me the pastor of a church. I knew my family problems would not be solved quickly but I knew also that the first step was to become a resident father. Within three months of my decision in Indiana I had done that.

As a father in residence I made many more mistakes as a dad and husband. But I was at home making those mistakes. Slowly we worked together to build not a perfect family but a stronger family. We picked up the pieces of our marriage and the Lord helped us to become truly one. And that bonding is still strong in the sunset years of our lives.

The lesson it took me forty years to learn is this: A man's family is more important than his career. The family should be a man's primary concern. If the pursuit of a successful career costs a man his family, his success will be hollow and little comfort to him in his old age. Fortunate is the man who learns this lesson in time to get his priorities in order. +

13

A beautiful gift everybody needs

She was lonely and bitter. When I asked her why she was so bitter she said simply, "Because I hate my mother." She went on to say, "I have not spoken to her for 27 years."

Her anger was understandable given the cruel way her mother had wronged her. But what struck me was the terrible result of the woman's unwillingness to forgive her mother.

She was a wretched, pitiful excuse for a human being. A prisoner of her own hatred, she was in bondage to a suffocating attitude that had robbed her of any semblance of joy. In a sense she was dead but her funeral had not yet been announced.

Months later, after much counseling and prayer, she chose to forgive her mother and their ruptured relationship was restored. The difference in the woman was startling. She was a new person, vibrantly alive, no longer trapped by her own bitterness. She had been set free from a prison of her own making. Her face was learning how to smile again.

If I have learned anything on my journey it is this: life is impossible without forgiveness. It is a beautiful gift that everyone needs. Everyone can give it. Everyone can receive it. Everyone is blessed when the gift of forgiveness is shared.

I like the way the author Frederick Buechner described the power of forgiveness. He said, "When somebody you have wronged forgives you, you are spared the dull and self-diminishing throb of a guilty conscience."

He is right. Guilt is like an anchor, grounding us at the point of our wrongdoing. Our life, like a ship, is not free to sail onward. A guilty conscience weakens us; the constant remembrance of what we did wrong squeezes the joy out of the daily routine.

Buechner explains well what happens when we take the initiative to forgive someone who has wronged us. He says, "When you forgive someone who has wronged you, you are spared the dismal corrosion of bitterness and wounded pride for both parties. Forgiveness means the freedom again to be at peace inside your own skin and to be glad in each other's presence."

The "dismal corrosion of bitterness" is indeed devastating and can actually destroy the person who refuses to forgive. The freedom to "be at peace within your own skin" is what restored life to the woman who finally forgave her mother. When she gave her mother the beautiful gift of forgiveness, she broke the chains of hatred with which she had bound herself.

There are people all around us who looking for forgiveness. Some need to be forgiven and some need to forgive someone who has wronged them.

I like the story of a Spanish father and son who were estranged. The son ran away and the distraught father tried to find him. Unable to find him the father put this ad in a Madrid newspaper: "Dear Paco, meet me in front of the newspaper office at noon on Saturday. All is forgiven. I love you. Your father."

That Saturday at noon, so the story goes, 800 Pacos showed up, looking for forgiveness and love from their fathers. The story is no doubt apocryphal but it does remind us of our common need for forgiveness.

Henry Ford was a brilliant inventor. Despite his brilliance he forgot to put a reverse gear in the first car he invented. What is even worse he did not build a door wide enough to get the car out of the building in which he built it. He had to cut a hole in the wall to get the car out.

If we refuse to give the beautiful gift of forgiveness to someone who has wronged us, we imprison ourselves. Then only a forgiving spirit can cut a hole in that prison and allow us to get out.

Forgiveness is really what the Christian faith is all about. Everybody has sinned. Sin enslaves us. God loves us anyway. He sent his son to tell us we are forgiven. His gift of forgiveness is offered us in the nail-scarred hands of Jesus. Only from those wounded hands may we receive it.

Receiving that gift we are set free from our sins. In that freedom we have peace with God – and that peace moves us to forgive those who have wronged us.

Forgiveness is a beautiful gift but it must be shared if we are to experience its transforming power. Receive it and share it because life is impossible without it. +

14

Times when we cry "Lord, I cannot"

My wife Dean introduced me to an old song that is new to me. The words and music were written by Jane LaRowe. I am learning it because I want to store it in my heart and sing it now and then.

Jane and I have become good friends through her song. Her words speak to my heart. Though I have never seen her I have spoken out loud to her. I said "Thank you Jane for touching my heart with your beautiful song." I think I heard her say "You are welcome."

Each of the four verses of Jane's song pictures an impossible situation about which Jane cries, "Lord, I cannot." There is a valley that is too deep, a mountain that is too high and a river that is too wide. And there is a pathway that she must travel alone.

Most of us have faced maddening times when in despair we cried out with Jane, "Lord, I cannot." There was a crisis we could not face, a problem we could not solve, a cruelty we could not endure. But about the time we were ready to jump off the nearest bridge and end it all, the Lord stepped in and helped us.

A popular chorus puts it this way: "He will make a way where there is no way." That's what Jane affirms in her song – that when you are at the end of your rope with nowhere to turn, the Lord comes to your rescue. And, praise God, he does just that!

Jane says that with the presence of the Lord she is able to walk through that deep valley "in His footsteps." He gives her "quiet strength" to scale the heights of that high mountain. On her lonely pathway she hears the Lord's voice and rejoices as he comes alongside her. And she gets across that wide river because he "takes her by the hand."

Life is a constant struggle, one fight after another. Just when you think you can relax and take it easy, calamity strikes again. But evidently that is God's game plan. He is not trying to make us "happy." He wants us to learn to depend on him so he can make us strong with character that glorifies him.

So the next time misfortune makes you cry, "Lord, I cannot," hang in there. Don't give up. Trust the Lord who loves you and believe with Jane LaRowe that with the Lord's help you can cross that deep valley and make it to the other side. You can – with His help! +

15

Celebrate no matter what is happening

One of my greatest blessings is that I am married to a woman who never stops celebrating. In the worst of times Dean has always found something to celebrate. And this is not a new behavior for her; it is a lifelong habit.

When our kids were small Dean greeted a rainy day with a smile. Instead of complaining because the boys could not go outside to play, she got them excited about games they could play inside. Her contagious enthusiasm soon convinced the boys that a rainy day was a blessing.

In one difficult season of our lives we struggled with multiple problems. No matter which way we turned we stepped in one pile of manure after another. One day she asked me, "Have you noticed how beautiful our roses are?"

I could have cared less about the roses. I was up to my eyeballs in alligators, desperately trying to get out of the mess we were in. That's when she said with a wry smile, "Those roses are thriving because of all the cow manure I packed around them. Manure helps roses to grow and we can let all the manure we are struggling with help us to grow too."

We started laughing and laughed until our faces were wet with tears. It was more than a teaching moment; it was a celebration that we have never forgotten. Since that day we have never allowed manure to overwhelm us. We simply look for ways to use it.

Dean's philosophy is that we should celebrate what is. Never give all your attention to what is broken; look for what is not broken and celebrate it. While life can be terribly difficult, if we look hard enough we can usually find a reason for hope. That hope may be but a glimmer of light in the darkness but we can celebrate it and look expectantly for the dawn that will surely come.

It is really a matter of attitude. While we often have no choice about our circumstances we can choose the attitude with which we face the situation. The control switch is on the inside; we can decide to be victims or we can decide to be victorious. The choice is ours.

Flexibility will help. Rigidity does not help. When problems are relentlessly punching us we can roll with the punch. When we are knocked down we can get up, brush ourselves off and get back in the race. We do not have to stay down.

We can choose to be happy even in hard times because happiness is a choice. We can learn to enjoy what we have rather than make ourselves miserable wishing for something we might not enjoy if we got it.

No groceries in the pantry? No cans of tuna or sardines? No problem for Dean. She celebrates the challenge of fixing a meal when there appears to be nothing to fix. One day she took the meat off the bones of two bream leftover from a recent supper. Then to the meat she added some onions, pickles and mayonnaise. Crackers and tea completed the menu. With a twinkle in her eye she said, "I pretended it was tuna fish salad and it was delicious!"

Her celebratory spirit inspired me to suggest that we really live it up and go out to Taco Bell for supper. Two celebrations in one day are not too many! After all I am not stingy; I am a big spender!

The lesson for the day: no matter what is happening you can find a way to celebrate! Celebrate what is. Celebrate what has been. Celebrate what is to come. With your last breath, celebrate! Some folks may think you are nuts, but when the last curtain falls you will have achieved the ultimate victory! +

16

An explosive idea

I enjoy dissecting a passage of scripture. One way to do that is to study several different translations. Often a beautiful new insight will jump out at me as modern words shed new light on old truths.

My copy of *The New Testament in Modern English* by J. B. Phillips is a bit tattered now. It was a gift from a dear friend and fellow pastor, Jim Connor. He wrote in the flyleaf kind words and thanked me "for being my Christian friend and companion in 'The Way' of Christ." The date was June 2, 1967.

Jim ran on ahead of us to the Father's House a few years ago. I hated to see him go but I know where he is and I plan to see him before long. I want to tell him again how much I have treasured his gift.

J. B. Phillips was an excellent preacher but his greatest gift to the world was his translation of the New Testament. He started translating the Old Testament but the Lord called him home before he could complete it. If he had finished translating the whole Bible I imagine it would have been called the "Phillips 66 Translation." (That's only funny if you remember how many books are in the Bible!)

Recently I had fun digging in the truth of Colossians 1:11-14. In any translation that is a powerful passage. I began my study by reflecting on the New International Version and found it a little cumbersome. See if you agree:

being strengthened with all power according to his glorious might so that you may have great endurance and patience, and joyfully giving thanks to the Father, who has qualified you to share in the inheritance of the saints in the kingdom of light. For he has rescued us from the dominion of darkness and brought us into the kingdom of the Son he loves, in whom we have redemption, the forgiveness of sins.

I underlined the striking words "endurance," "patience," "joy-fully," "rescued," and "forgiveness." With these significant words Paul is showing us how to pray for one another.

Then I turned to J. B. Phillips and my heart began to sing as I read his version:

As you live this new life, we pray that you will be strengthened from God's boundless resources, so that you will find yourselves able to pass through an experience and endure it with joy. You will even be able to thank God in the midst of pain and distress because you are privileged to share the lot of those who are living in the light. For we must never forget that he rescued us from the power of darkness, and reestablished us in the kingdom of his beloved Son. For it is by his Son alone that we have been redeemed and have had our sins forgiven.

My eyes fastened on the words "pass through an experience and endure it with joy." I got excited. The concept of "passing through" a hardship is good theology. When times are tough we want grace to get "through the night" rather than get stranded in the pain. In the 23rd Psalm David speaks of walking "through" the valley of the shadow of death. My heart says Yes! This tells me that God wants to help us "pass through" a hardship and get victory over it.

But the best phrase of all is the next one. Phillips has Paul praying that we will not only pass through a hardship but "endure it with joy." I underlined those words twice! This is a new way to suffer misfortune – to do so with joy! The word "endure" had always conjured up the idea of tolerating a problem, suffering through it, and gritting your teeth to the bitter end. But Phillips injects "joy" into the ordeal!

That marvelous idea was suddenly lit up on the billboard of my soul – God can help me endure difficulty with joy! I want that kind of faith. I have some of it. I want more! I need more!

Well, that is one example of what can happen when, with an open mind, you begin searching for truth in the Holy Scriptures! +

17

The difference between winning and losing

Winners choose the right attitude. No matter what your circumstances you have the freedom to choose the attitude with which you will respond. This is one of the great privileges of life.

When bad and crazy things happen you can remain calm or go berserk. Your attitude makes all the difference in whether you are a winner or a loser. When a storm develops you can seek shelter and enjoy the change of pace or you can curse the sky and assume a hurricane will follow the storm.

One day a pigeon dropped a load on my shirt. I told my wife it must be raining. She died laughing and said, "It is not raining. A pigeon just pooped on you!" I laughed too, wiped the mess off my shirt and told her, "Well, even pigeons have to go the bathroom sometime."

I could have moaned for an hour that I was probably the only man in Pensacola who got drilled by a pigeon that day. But it would have done no good to cry, "Why me?" That would have made me a loser. I chose to be a winner by not allowing a reckless little pigeon to ruin my day. And pigeon poop does not smell all that bad anyway.

My wife loves Matthew Henry. I mean she loves his commentary on the Bible. Henry was an Englishman and a Presbyterian preacher. He died suddenly at age 52 in 1714 but before his death he had written a marvelous commentary on the entire Bible. His exposition of the scriptures is still remarkably helpful despite its age. A few years ago I bought my wife Henry's one-volume commentary on the Bible; it weighs about five pounds.

I love the story about the time Henry was accosted by thieves who robbed him of his money. Here is how he reacted: "Let me be thankful first because I was never robbed before; second, although they took my purse, they did not take my life; third, because, although they took my all, it was not much; and fourth, because it was I who was robbed, not I who robbed another." What a winning attitude!

My friend Paul Duffey, a fellow Methodist preacher who was also a bishop, had a winning attitude. I never heard him complain about adverse circumstances, even the death of his dear wife Louise. I remember hearing Paul say, "Adversity will often color our lives – but we can choose the color!" Paul chose a winning attitude until the Lord called him home at age 91.

Whatever your circumstances just now, resist the temptation to wallow in self-pity and complain about your misfortune. To whine is to choose the wrong color. So choose to be thankful for the blessings you enjoy. The right perspective can make you a winner. +

18

A daddy whose love children can remember

I am a blessed man. I had a daddy who loved me. He loved me for a long time, until he died at age 93.

Daddy was seldom tender. But despite his lack of gentleness I never doubted that he loved me. His discipline was often harsh but never so harsh that I questioned his love for me. Looking back I believe I deserved every scolding and every lick he ever gave me.

It grieves me that so many children must grow up without the loving presence of a daddy in the home. God's plan for the family is still the best one: children should be raised in a home by a mother and a father.

The absence of a caring father can be devastating to a child. Lewis Grizzard used to speak and write about his daddy with such pathos. His stories were filled with humor but flavored with sadness.

In his book, *My Daddy Was a Pistol and I'm a Son of a Gun*, Grizzard shares how he had such little time together with his father. "War took him away," he says. "Then he came back for a short time before he was gone again." And because his father never returned on a fulltime basis, Grizzard treasured every memory of his dad.

Grizzard shares that while he had some pictures of his father, his Bronze Star and his Purple Hearts, "what I don't have any more is him." And he writes with heartrending sorrow, "That is why I remember, and cherish, the memories of the man's hair, his smell, his likes and dislikes, his speech, and his idiosyncrasies."

The gifted Grizzard felt deeply the loss of growing up without a loving father in his life. But Lewis did have his daddy with him during some of his childhood; many children never know even once the comfort of being rocked to sleep in the arms of their father.

The writer Philip Yancey tells a touching story from his own life in his book, *Disappointment with God*. Yancey's father died when Philip was barely a year old. On a visit with his widowed mother, Yancy tells how the two of them spent an afternoon looking through old photos. She showed him a picture of Philip when he was only eight months old. The picture was tattered and Yancey wondered why his mother had kept it.

"My mother explained to me," Yancey writes, "that she had kept the photo as a memento because during my father's illness it had been fastened to his iron lung." Yancey learned that during the last few months of his father's life he had lain on his back, paralyzed by polio at age 24, and now encased from the neck down in a huge breathing machine. His young sons were not allowed in the hospital so Yancey's father asked for pictures of the boys.

The photos were jammed between metal knobs and hung within view above him – the only thing he could see since he could not move his head. He spent the last four months of his miserable life looking at the faces of the sons he loved.

What a revelation this must have been to Yancey. His insight is profoundly touching. This is his moving response: "I have often thought of that crumpled photo, for it is one of the few links connecting me to the stranger who was my father. Someone I have no memory of, no sensory knowledge of, spent all day, every day thinking of me, devoting himself to me, loving me . . . The emotions I felt when my mother showed me the crumpled photo were the very same emotions I felt that February night in a college dorm room when I first believed in a God of love. Someone is there, I realized. Someone is there who loves me. It was a startling feeling of wild hope, a feeling so new and overwhelming that it seemed fully worth risking my life on."

That crumpled photo helped Philip Yancey to realize he did have a father whose love he could remember – and he was incredibly blessed by that awareness.

Every child needs a daddy whose love they can remember. Wise is the father who does his best to "be there" for his children. What is needed is not perfection but presence wrapped up in love. +

19

Wear a morning face

At my age every new morning is a marvelous blessing. Though I don't bounce out of bed I do rejoice to see the morning light. My old bones move rather slowly now but I can still walk on my own. On my doctor's advice I stand still on my feet for a few seconds before starting the walk to the bathroom. He says this allows my blood to start circulating and will help me to avoid falling.

My wife and I are early risers. I reckon old folks just don't require much sleep. My coffee is perking a little after six most mornings and we are both eager to start the new day.

I do my best to match the pleasant disposition of my sweet wife. She greets every morning cheerfully. Dean is a convert of the writer Robert Louis Stevenson who admonished people to get up with a happy face, what he called "a morning face and a morning heart."

Stevenson is one of the people I wish I had known. He died too soon. Born in Edinburgh, Scotland in 1850, he died of a stroke in 1894. His 44 years were wonderfully productive. His books are treasured worldwide. You remember that he was the author of *Treasure Island*, *Kidnapped* and *Dr. Jekyll and Mr. Hyde*. He also wrote excellent poetry.

If I could talk to Stevenson I would tell him how much his poetry has meant to me but especially to my wife. For years she has blessed audiences by reciting Stevenson's delightful poem titled "The Swing." Dean adores the poem for its charming cadence and its enthusiasm for life. But she loves it even more because it was written by a man who remained cheerful in the midst of his suffering.

Stevenson struggled with various illnesses all his life. He was so sick during his early years that he was unable to attend school as a regular student until age 14. When 26 he married Fanny, a divorcee with two children, who also suffered from poor health. Despite her own health problems Fanny devotedly nursed Robert until his death.

Robert and Fanny lived in several countries, including France and America, but fell in love with the climate in the Pacific. So in 1890 they settled in Samoa where he continued writing and became known and loved by the Samoans. They called him "Tusitala," a writer of tales. The brief four years in Samoa were the happiest years of their lives.

A victim of tuberculosis, Robert refused to surrender to despair and self-pity. He rose above his pain and maintained a positive attitude. One of his stepdaughters, Isobel Field, described Stevenson's victorious spirit in a book of her own, *This Life I've Loved.*

Isobel wrote, "One day Stevenson read us a prayer he had just written. In it were words none of us will ever forget:

'When the day returns, call us up with morning faces and morning hearts, eager to labor, happy if happiness be our portion, and if the day be marked for sorrow, strong to endure.'

Isobel continued: "We awakened on the morrow with happy morning faces, but that day was marked for sorrow. That day, at the height of his fame, in the best of health he had ever enjoyed, Louis went out of this life suddenly, quietly, painlessly."

When I am tempted to be grouchy in the morning, it helps to remember Stevenson's indomitable courage and his resolve to wear a cheerful morning face. The world needs more people with morning faces and morning hearts. I think I shall try to be such a person until the Lord calls me home. +

Please enjoy "The Swing" one more time:

How do you like to go up in a swing,
Up in the air so blue?
Oh, I do think it the pleasantest thing
Ever a child can do!

Up in the air and over the wall,
Till I can see so wide,
Rivers and trees and cattle and all
Over the countryside—

Till I look down on the garden green,
Down on the roof so brown—
Up in the air I go flying again,
Up in the air and down!
(A Child's Garden of Verses, 1999)

20

Eating at a table

Some say the wheel is the greatest of all inventions. That may be true but I believe the invention of the table ranks in the top ten. A table where two or more people can sit and eat is surely a marvelous thing.

My love of tables began in my childhood. My earliest and most cherished memories have to do with eating at a table with my siblings and my parents. Daddy built what we called "the breakfast table" with his own hands and it is one of my most prized possessions. The old table is more beautiful than ever now, having been given new life recently by dear friends Alan Brewer and Jim Rush.

There was a place for each of us at the table. We sat at the same place at every meal. And we never began eating until Daddy had prayed the only prayer I ever heard him pray: "Bless, O Lord, this food to our use and ourselves to thy service. For Christ's sake, Amen."

We were taught the habit of washing our hands before meals. And you dared not sit down at Daddy's table with a cap on your head. Daddy did not waste words about the cap. He would simply slap it off your head. The sting of that abrupt removal would help you remember not to wear your cap to the table again.

Lest you judge Daddy too harshly let me tell you that my siblings and I came to be thankful for Daddy's stern ways. He taught us to respect the rules of the house. He gave us a sense of reverence for the table, for family mealtimes and for the food we shared. Looking back, I realize now that for Daddy there was something sacred about sitting at the table and sharing a meal as a family.

The table has a prominent place in the Bible. The Psalmist David spoke tenderly of how the Lord had prepared a table before him "in the presence of his enemies." Jesus sat at tables with sinners to demonstrate his acceptance of them.

Then there is the table in the upper room where Jesus sat and ate "the last supper" with his disciples the night before his crucifixion. Ever since that time his followers have gathered around a table, a communion table, to share the Eucharist or the holy meal.

During December the table in our home is beautifully decorated with candles and Christmas colors. Most years my wife will set up four tables so we can entertain her beloved Sunday school class for lunch. We enjoy the food but even more the fellowship with dear Christian friends.

After the meal we enjoy coffee and cake and sing Christmas carols with Dot Nichols playing the piano. Dot is in her nineties but she can still play and we love to hear her play. We talk and listen and care for one another, celebrating being alive and being together.

Life in the fast lane is exciting for the young but for those of us in the golden years there are few things more satisfying than gathering around a table to share a meal with friends. Surely friendships are strengthened – and family relationships as well – when we put our feet under a table and take the time to enjoy good food and good conversation.

The table – what a great invention! +

21

Doorway to a new beginning

Disappointment comes to everyone. Life is not fair. Things do not work out the way we hoped they would. Dreams shatter. Failure happens.

Bob and Betty were madly in love. They got married, had three children and planned to live happily ever after. Along the way Bob neglected Betty. He became a slave to his work. Betty walked out one day. She was in love with another man. Bob sat crying in the ashes of disappointment.

Bill's father was a preacher. Bill's mother encouraged him to follow in his dad's footsteps. Bill became a preacher but found peace in ministry. One day he realized his mother, not God, had called him to preach. Crushed and disappointed Bill quit the ministry and began teaching school.

Tom went off to college with high hopes. Six months later he was not on the Dean's list; he had flunked out. Ashamed and disappointed he wiped his tears and got a job driving a milk truck. His dream of a college degree was gone with the wind. He was devastated and enveloped by an ugly cloud of regret.

Mary wanted to become an artist. She loved to draw and paint. Friends encouraged her to study art. But there was no money to go to school. She got married, had five children and buried her dream in the black pit of disappointment. Her dream shattered she clung to the slim hope that one of her kids might become an artist.

Pete felt no need to go to college. After high school he went to work at his dad's company. He would work hard and take over the business one day. Nine years later his dad died suddenly. The new owner of the business had no need for Pete. He downsized the company and let

Pete go. Without a job Pete struggled to find his way out of the misery of disappointment.

Charles and Linda were devoted to each other. Linda had a beautiful baby boy. They named him Frank and he became the center of their lives. When Frank was 17 he was killed in a car wreck. Charles began drinking heavily and soon left Linda for a younger woman. For years now Linda has lived like a recluse, her mind filled with anger and bitterness. Disappointment has enslaved her.

King David, the Bible tells us, dreamed of building a temple to honor God. He intended to do it one day but he stayed busy going to war. He loved to fight and was good at it. Then one day God informed David that he would not build a temple; instead his son Solomon would build it. God was not pleased with David's love of wars. David's disappointment was overwhelming.

But somehow David found a way to overcome his disappointment. He refused to quit. He refused to live the rest of his life nursing bitterness. Call it trust. Call it faith. Call it turning to God. Call it what you will – David found a way to move out of the paralyzing fog of disappointment and start over.

What helped David we call grace today. When the bottom falls out of life, when our dreams are shattered by pain and disappointment, we can turn to our Creator for grace. He has plenty of it, enough to go around so everyone can have some. He will give it graciously to all who ask for it. Disappointment is real but grace is more real.

The next time disappointment seizes you by the throat, tell it to go back to hell where it came from. Then avail yourself of the grace you need to make a new start. That way you can make disappointment the door to a new beginning. I know you can do it because I have done it more than once. And more than likely I will have to do it again. And, by the grace of God, I will.

You can do it too. Now get up and get started. Now. This minute. When you make a new start, you cease being a victim and become a victor! Disappointment makes you a wimp. Grace makes you a winner. You get to decide which you will be! +

22

When the bottom falls out

Calamity happens. It may be of your own making. It may be the result of a natural disaster like a tornado. Or your misfortune may have been caused by other people. But whatever the source of your trouble you must respond to it – unless you have decided to throw in the towel.

So the question is this: what is the best way to respond when the bottom falls out of your world? Let's think this through together.

First, react as wisely as you possibly can. You are in control of your reactions; you cannot control the actions or reactions of others. Be careful that you do not overreact. To do so will usually make matters worse and bring on later the pain of regret.

Second, to react wisely may require that you step back from your trouble and ask yourself some hard questions: Am I responsible for the trouble I am in? Am I at fault? If your trouble is mostly of your own making, then repent and seek forgiveness. If forgiveness is not forthcoming, at least you tried. The process of repentance and forgiveness includes forgiving yourself. All of us make mistakes; no one is perfect. Jesus gave us no beatitude that says, "Blessed are those who despise themselves." Self-despising is a dead-end street.

Third, take the initiative to make things right with anyone you may have offended or wronged. Now and then someone may not forgive you; their reaction is out of your control. But at least, ask for forgiveness. Until you do that you will not be able to move on with your life.

Fourth, if you are angry at someone (or yourself) be smart enough to put your anger aside. Anger will not help things get better; it will definitely make things worse. To be angry about our troubles is to be stupid. So do not be stupid. Anger leads us into the blame game;

blaming others for our misfortunes is another dead-end street. Blaming someone else is always counter-productive.

Fifth, consider all your options carefully and choose to do the right thing, one step at a time. Do what is right for others; do what is right for you. You are never wrong to do what is right. Respond to your troubles with integrity. You will never be embarrassed for choosing the pathway of integrity. React with honor and truthfulness. Do the honorable thing one day at a time – for the rest of your life.

Sixth, seek the counsel of good friends. Pain can cloud our vision. Friends can help us see the best way to go. You must make your own decisions but you will be wise to test your conclusions with others whose judgment you trust. Good friends will never guide you in the wrong direction.

Seventh, take time to think through your dilemma but beware of procrastination. While you should not rush into important decisions, remember that pain sometimes results in inertia. If that happens you may need to take yourself by the nap of the neck and get back in the game. Nothing good ever comes out of lethargy. Inaction produces no positive change.

Eighth, get on your knees and ask the God who loves you and is always in your corner to give you the grace to face your trouble squarely and then get over it and move on! Life is not over as long as you are still breathing. The God who created you is more ready to help you that you ever dreamed. So let him help you! Choose to believe that God's plans for you are good! When you decide to love God more than anything else in this world, things and people begin to fall in place in your life.

Ninth, get up every day and remind yourself that the God who guides the sun and the moon in their orbits is willing to guide you into a new life of meaning, joy and peace. He can do it. He will do it – if you ask him! If doubt makes you question this, then do what I do often. I start singing an old song that soon chases my doubts away. It goes like this, "Guide me, O thou great Jehovah, pilgrim through this barren land. I am weak, but thou are mighty; hold me with thy powerful hand. Bread of heaven, feed me till I want no more; feed me till I want no more." It works for me!

Tenth, never give up. Never give up on yourself. Never give up on God. Never give up on the wisdom of doing the right thing again and again. Never give up on the future. Never give up on your potential. Never give up on your power to make lemonade with your lemons. When the bottom falls out a cool glass of lemonade can help you handle the pressure while you decide what to do next.

You are not the first person who had to start over. Wounded people have made new beginnings since the world began. So stop babbling and take charge of your life. And never forget that God is using the pain and trouble of this world to prepare you, and the rest of us, for something better! +

23

Moving beyond rejection

Rejection can be hell. It has the power to bring down the best of us. It can handcuff us, demoralize us and cause us to give up. Whether we admit it or not the affirmation of other people is a basic need of all normal people. To lose the acceptance of the people who are important to you is always devastating.

Condemnation from people you love is no doubt the worst kind of rejection. Few people can live well without the encouragement and support of at least one or two friends. Yet some of us are ready to denounce the bad behavior of a person who has developed the habit of failure. And our rejection can push the struggling person deeper into the pit of despair.

Climbing out of the hell hole of rejection is never easy; and it is usually impossible without the help of someone with the gift of mercy. That "someone" can be God whose mercy is fresh every morning. The person who has failed morally must first seek and embrace God's forgiveness. This is true because our sins are first and foremost "against God," as King David said, even though people are hurt by our sins. And to find lasting peace, after accepting God's mercy, we must also ask forgiveness from those persons harmed by our sins.

So how does a person recover from rejection and move on? First, realize that everybody fails at one time or another. No one is perfect. Failure is part of the fabric of life. It will help to acknowledge that you have failed and may truly deserve the pain of rejection. But your life is not over as long as you have the breath to make a new start.

You have another choice. You can forgive yourself, accept God's forgiveness and seek the forgiveness of those hurt by your failure. Then you can get up and walk on! You need not wallow in the misery and self-pity of your pain and disappointment. You can start over again!

Remind yourself that you are not the first person to be rejected for failing. Read a bit of history and note how many others failed but found the courage to begin again. They leaped over rejection. The list is endless. Thomas Edison failed hundreds of times but he refused to quit trying. Babe Ruth had almost twice as many strikeouts as he did home runs. The Ford Motor Company gave us the Edsel, a colossal failure, but the company is still producing Ford cars and trucks.

Winston Churchill failed the sixth grade and lost many elections but he kept bouncing back until he became Prime Minister of England. Beethoven's teacher said he was hopeless; now his nameless teacher is known only for that glaring mistake! Albert Einstein could not read until he was seven and his teacher described him as "mentally slow." Walt Disney was fired for "a lack of ideas" and went bankrupt several times before creating Disneyland.

Refuse to say "I am a failure." Instead admit that you are a person who has failed. Though you have failed you need not sit and whine; you can rise up and walk into a new future. The God who created you will help you. Take Him at his word: "When you seek me with all your heart you will find me."

If the important people in your life have given up on you, forgive them and move on. Refuse to give up on yourself. Find one or two other people who will believe in you and encourage you to recover. Care about them. Do kind things for them. Get busy making a difference in their lives. The more you do that, the less time you will have to fret about the past. Bury your pain and make a new start! Graves are useful; dig one for your rejection. Pain can be beneficial if it spurs you to make a new beginning!

Someone once described the Christian life like this: "We fall down and we get up, we fall down and we get up, and we keep falling down and getting up all the way to heaven!" That is how I see it too. So what is keeping you down? Get up and go again! Then one day soon your fresh new joy will be far more real than the pain of failure and rejection and there will be a smile on your face instead of tears on your cheeks. Go for it! +

24

Many voices clamor for our attention

Admit you "hear voices" in your mind and people may think you are strange. Some serial killers have blamed their violence on "voices" in their head. But strange as it may seem, many Christians claim to hear a voice that guides and comforts them.

At the risk of your concluding that I am odd I admit that I am such a Christian. For more than 60 years I have heard a voice within my mind and heart. I was in my mid-twenties when I heard the evangelist E. Stanley Jones talk about listening to what he called "the Inner Voice."

It was a new concept for me but I seized it as a fresh new way of relating to God. That day I began earnestly to listen to and obey the Inner Voice of Jesus. Though I have not always fully obeyed the guidance I heard, I can testify that the Inner Voice has never given me bad counsel. Whenever I have obeyed I have been blessed. And the more I have heard, the more I have wanted to hear, not so much with my ears as with my heart and soul.

Jones helped me to believe that when the Inner Voice speaks he is always wise, practical and sensible. It was Jones' habit to rise early every morning and spend time at his "listening post." One morning, though he was dogged tired from having slept only a couple of hours that night, he dragged himself out of bed to keep his appointment with the Inner Voice. With a grin Jones said the Voice told him to go back to bed and get some more sleep! I find it easy to trust a God like that!

On my journey I have found the guidance of the Inner Voice to be consistent with the teachings of Jesus in the Bible. That is not surprising because the Inner Voice and Jesus are one and the same. But

I do believe it important to constantly test the teaching of the Inner Voice with the teaching of the Holy Scriptures. The Inner Voice actually counsels me to do that and doing so helps me avoid confusing His Voice with some of the other inner "voices" clamoring for my attention.

My decision to listen to the Inner Voice was further confirmed by the marvelous Quaker writer D. Elton Trueblood. Speaking in a conference in Oklahoma City Elton offered a profound definition of a Christian. He said that a Christian is someone who "hears many voices" amidst the noise and confusion of the world but "One Voice" gets his attention. That is the voice of Jesus Christ. Listening to and obeying that voice the Christian begins to "know the joy of being used for a mighty purpose by which his little life is dignified." As he spoke I felt my heart pounding Yes, Yes, and Yes!

In recent years I have been blessed by the writing of the eminent theologian N. T. Wright. He too urges Christians to listen to the voice of God and obey it as best they can. Wisely, Wright advises us that the one place where we can be sure to hear the voice of God is "in the cry of those in need." That has been true for me. I have often heard the Inner Voice speak directly to me through the cries of the poor, especially hurting widows and orphans.

What have I heard the Inner Voice say to me? You can figure that out rather quickly; he tells me the same things he tells any sinner who is listening! Sometimes he says quietly, "You were wrong; repent, apologize, and ask forgiveness from those you offended." And unless and until I obey his voice, he says nothing else. His silence is a great motivator so I get busy trying to obey.

At other times he affirms me, reminding me that I am loved despite my sins and as long as I am willing, he is willing to let me do things that will bring joy and dignity to my little life. Now and then he grants me the great joy of knowing that I was in the right place at the right time doing what he wanted me to do.

More than anything I constantly hear him whispering, "I am with you. I am your Lord. I will help you as long as you lean on me. Keep listening to me and you will not go astray. Look every day for ways to help your brothers and sisters who are in need. I will give you the grace you need to do my will. And never forget that in spite of your weaknesses, I love you. You are mine and I am yours, now and forever."

Hearing such a voice makes me glad to be alive despite the pain and heartache of this broken world. And every day I pray for the courage to keep saying as long as I have breath, "Yes, Lord, whatever you say!" +

25

There's just got to be another morning!

Years ago when we lived in Mobile a neighbor's little girl was killed in an automobile accident. I think she was seven. She was a beautiful child. Our young sons often played with her and other children in the neighborhood.

The child's sudden death in a freak wreck at an intersection shocked and saddened us. Though we were not close friends with the family my wife and I decided to attend the funeral at a nearby church. The church was filled with friends and family members who came to share the sorrow of the grieving family.

What I remember most about the funeral was a solo sung by a young woman. I had never heard the song before but it seemed perfect for the occasion. The words still etched in my mind are these: "There's got to be another morning!" That was the theme of the song: because of the pain and sadness of life, there's got be another morning.

I wept as I listened and kept saying in my mind, "Yes! Yes! That's right! There's just got to be another morning!" That beautiful girl had only begun to live. Her life was cut short. So there just has to be another morning when bad things are made right, when the unfinished can finally be completed. Surely her tragic death is not the end; there simply has to be more, thus the plaintive hope for "another morning."

In the face of the heartbreaking death of a child the human spirit longs for, even cries for more. The cynic does not share this longing. Life is not fair, he says; the grave is the end so accept it and get on with your life. But hope lives on in the hearts of others who cling to the conviction that a loving God provides for life beyond the grave.

That is one reason why I believe in the resurrection. Surely God has another plan for a beautiful life that is snuffed out at age seven. Surely his plans include the completion of lovely things that are not finished in this earthly life. Surely God who is the author of life is able to finish on the other side what he so beautifully began on this side.

Question my conclusion if you must but I am persuaded that at last, whenever God brings down the curtain, the crooked will be made straight. Darkness will be overcome by the light. Goodness will prevail over evil. Life will conquer death. Love will win in the end; hate will lose. Though God allows evil to have its day, ultimately right will triumph over wrong. Righteousness will finally defeat wickedness.

I believe in the resurrection because it was necessary for God to complete what he began in Jesus. Death, hell and the grave had to give way to the power of God. He raised his son Jesus from the grave so he could complete the gracious plan of redemption. Alive once again, Jesus gathered his disciples and commissioned them to make known the plan of salvation for the world.

Confronted by the resurrected Christ, the apostles could hardly believe what had happened – but they did believe it. They saw Jesus die on the cross. Then they saw him alive, raised from the dead by the power of God. They did as Jesus told them and soon were filled with a strange new power themselves. The same divine power that raised Jesus from the dead filled the disciples with new life, joy and hope. They began spreading the word – "He's alive!"

Down the centuries since then that good news has continued to spread. Millions have believed the testimony of those early disciples and have continued to pass along the message – "He's alive!"

On every Easter day that message is proclaimed on every continent as more and more people believe and celebrate the resurrection of Jesus and his promise of eternal life to his followers. Then one day the end will come and Jesus will return to judge the world. At that time there will be another morning, a glorious morning when God will finish the unfinished. I believe it. There has just got to be another morning – because He's alive! +

26

Faith helps us rejoice in hard times

My sisters asked me, "How did our parents afford to send us to college?" They were not wealthy. Income from our small farm was modest one year and poor the next.

We concluded that "sacrifice" was the only reasonable explanation. Our parents sacrificed for us. They denied themselves so their children could get an education. And long since they left this world, we are still thankful for their sacrifice.

In the fifties, my father faced hard times despite his sacrifice for his children. He had to forfeit some land he had bought. Money was tight. Debts were piled high. Without whimpering, dad accepted a job as the manager of the county farmers' exchange. Now he could make ends meet. He would continue what farming he could on a part-time basis. I never heard him complain. Instead he maintained a positive spirit. He worked hard – from daylight till dark – not for himself but for his family.

I know now that he did not complain because he trusted a mighty God, the kind of God the prophet Habakkuk trusted. The kind of God he could believe in even when the fields yielded no fruit!

When the illness of our first child resulted in back-breaking medical expenses for me and my wife, dad and mom rescued us with food and as much money as they could spare. Dad said, "We will do everything we can to help you." And they did.

Dad was a man of few words. Often those words were blunt. But he was a man of integrity. His word was his bond. If he told you something, you could count on it.

His family knew that he had backbone. His life was never easy. He worked hard all his life. But he never questioned or doubted God. His faith grew stronger as he grew older.

I think he had strength like that of Habakkuk. To pronounce correctly the prophet's name, you must use the word "back." So you pronounce his name "Huh-back-kuk." In his back was a strong, God-given backbone! It was not made of Jell-O.

The prophet saw hard times coming. God was going to punish the people for their sins. But Habakkuk's faith was not shaken. Indeed he believed God was in control, and nothing would be able to destroy the joy that God gives to his children who trust Him.

The little word "yet" is a powerful word. God's people are "Yet People." No matter how difficult the times, God's people are able to say, "Yet I will rejoice in the Lord, I will joy in the God of my salvation."

Hallelujah! May God give us in our day a backbone like that of my dad, and like that of Habakkuk – so that no disaster can shake us loose from a faith grounded in the joy of the Lord. +

27

Night will end and morning will come

If the Bible tells us anything it tells us that God hears the cries of his children. And that is good news when you are distressed. Trouble often seems like night so we speak of times that seem like the "dark night of the soul."

In the midst of such dark nights we are prone to think that God has deserted us, that he does not care about our misery. Darkness can seem heavy and breathing laborious. But somehow we cling to the hope that morning will come. That hope, though weak, enables us "to make it through the night."

Daylight is a welcome sight. It has always been so. That is how it was in the days of the prophet Jeremiah. Jerusalem had been destroyed. Most of the people were now exiles and slaves in a foreign land. Some were allowed to remain in Jerusalem where Jeremiah sought to help them understand the ways of the Lord.

Overwhelmed by sorrow, uprooted from their homeland, the Israelites had little hope for the future. They had disobeyed God. Now they were enduring God's punishment for their sins. Most of us know from experience what that feels like.

Despite the stubbornness of the Jews, God did not abandon them. God never stopped loving them. In fact, just when they needed it the most, God gave them the precious gift of hope. This gift was "made flesh" in a man – the prophet Jeremiah.

Jeremiah saw beyond the present suffering; he saw a future full of the goodness of God. The prophet saw that hope is greater than grief, that joy is greater than sorrow. Jeremiah knew that no matter how dark the night morning will come. And wisely the prophet linked "morning" with the grace of God.

Few greater visions of God are recorded in Holy Scripture than this one from the pen of the weeping prophet:

Because of the LORD's great love we are not consumed,
for his compassions never fail.
They are new every morning;
great is your faithfulness.
I say to myself, "The LORD is my portion;
therefore I will wait for him."
(Lamentations 3:22-24, NIV)

It was this vision that birthed the greatly beloved hymn, "Great is Thy Faithfulness." This soul-stirring song often brings me to my knees in worship, especially the words, "All I have needed, Thy Hand hath provided." I want to cry out for all to hear, "Yes, Lord, Yes! Glory!"

What a great truth for us to embrace and live by: God's mercies are new every morning! No matter what pain or misfortune we endured during the night, God's mercies are as sure as the morning light, and ours for the asking.

We may choose either the word "new" or "fresh" to describe his mercies. Both are beautiful words, though I prefer "fresh."

Morning suggests breakfast. When we rise from a night's rest, normally we feel renewed; we have fresh energy. The aroma of fresh coffee makes many of us glad to be alive.

Fresh bread smells so good and tastes delicious. Think of our disappointment if all we had for breakfast was day-old coffee and stale bread! No so God's mercies; they are fresh every morning!

Stanley Jones was being shown to his room at a retreat center. His hostess was a cheerful Roman Catholic nun who provided him with towels and soap. Politely she asked if there was anything else he needed.

With a twinkle in his eye the famous evangelist replied, "More grace." Smiling, the alert and witty nun responded: "Help yourself, Brother Stanley, it's all around you!"

She was right because God is faithful and he keeps His promises.

Our troubles may weigh us down, but we need not stay down. Whenever we will, we can reach out and help ourselves to the mercies of God.

Faith helps us believe that God's eye is "upon the sparrow," and thus upon me, and you, and all his children. He cares about our sorrows. He hurts when we hurt. And every new morning can be a new beginning because his compassion never fails!

Shout it until you believe it with all your heart, mind and soul: "The night will end and morning will come! Yes it will! Yes!" And never forget that mercy is the reason why! +

28

Love means never giving up on someone

My friend Bob made a lot of wrong choices growing up. As a high school student he ignored the curfew set by his parents, often coming home late at night "drunk as a hoot owl."

You may think that Bob's father reacted strangely to his son's wayward behavior. He never responded with anger or chastisement. Instead, no matter how late Bob stayed out at night, he always found his father fully dressed, sitting in a chair waiting for him to come home.

"When I came in, sometimes staggering, Dad never dressed me down," Bob said. "He simply helped me to bed, always patting me on the back as he said calmly, 'you'll be a fine man one day, son.'"

He was right. One day Bob quit running from God, gave up drinking, and was profoundly converted. More than a fine man, Bob became a new man in Christ. He went on to college, finished seminary and became an excellent teacher of the Christian faith.

Bob ought to understand the gospel. He experienced it. His own father introduced him to the God who never gives up on his children despite their wrong choices. I tremble with joy every time I hear Bob share his story. It underscores for me the true nature of God. He is the God of second chances.

Sin leads inexorably to suffering. When we insist on having our own way, defiantly refusing to obey God, we are on the pathway to suffering. None of us can get away with mocking God. He allows us to reap what we sow, to experience the pain of disobedience. We cannot break covenant with God without suffering the sad consequences he permits.

The Israelites of the Bible are a good example. They refused to put God first. They embraced pagan gods. They mocked the prophets God sent to turn them from their wicked ways. They scoffed at the goodness of God until finally they had to endure the wrath of God. The Chaldeans were allowed to be the instruments of God's wrath.

Grief accompanies suffering. The Judahites were overwhelmed with sadness because of the exile. They sat down by the riverside and wept bitter tears, unable to "sing the Lord's song in a foreign land." Their harps collected dust while they mourned for their loss. They only realized how much Jerusalem, the holy city, meant to them after they had lost it. How true that remains for us today!

When we are engulfed by the consequences of our own wrong choices, we can sit down and weep – or we can learn some valuable lessons about ourselves and God. When we scoff at the moral laws of God, we are spitting into the wind! We are sliding down the banisters of life with all the splinters pointed at us! When we break God's commandments we are really breaking ourselves! Would to God that the pain of our sins could teach us once and for all that life will work in only one way and that is the way of the Lord!

When we are suffering, as the result of our behavior, nothing can cheer us more than the good news of the gospel. The good news is that while we were still sinners, God showed his love for us by letting Jesus die for our sins. The good news is that God never stops loving us! He never gives up on his children.

Wise parents allow their children to suffer the consequences of their behavior but they never stop loving them. Even when they come in late at night drunk, loving parents will offer them a second chance, and a third, and a fourth, to get it right!

Hard times, brought on by my own wrong choices, have taught me repeatedly that I cannot mock God without suffering severe consequences. It was during such hard times that I begged for mercy, turned from my wicked ways, and went running to my Father – always sure that he was ready to give me another chance to get my life right!

Today we who love Christ have no greater joy than to tell those who are running from God by mocking all that is pure, noble and true that God will never give up on them. His transforming love awaits their turning to him for a second chance! +

29

Every worthy endeavor requires persistence

We hear it said that great deeds are the result of blood, sweat and tears. Well for my money you can forget the tears. What every worthy endeavor requires is actually blood, sweat and persistence. Few things worth doing are ever accomplished without persistence. It is the great secret to success.

This virtue of the human spirit calls to mind words like diligence, doggedness, unrelenting, determination and perseverance. These words remind us that unless we are willing to "keep on keeping on," often against overwhelming resistance, our efforts will not be crowned with success.

The Bible offers us many excellent examples, not the least of which is the unrelenting pursuit of the will of God by Jesus. But for a moment consider the example of Nehemiah. He took on a difficult assignment for God. It was a task he could not accomplish alone. The rebuilding of the wall required the help of many people. Some of the people he called on to help let him down. But Nehemiah refused to give up. He stayed the course.

Churches sometime fall to pieces when disgruntled people walk away from the fellowship. Those members who remain must decide whether to give up or carry on. Recovery usually requires a few people with the spirit of Nehemiah who will, without rancor toward the quitters, persist in finding other people to join them in getting the job done. If you say of some person you admire, "He stayed the course," you have paid that person a beautiful compliment.

Nehemiah's noble efforts were fiercely opposed. But he did not allow his detractors to defeat him. He used the gifts God had given him – the gifts of persuasion, organization, encouragement and faith in God. He persuaded people to embrace his vision. He organized the people according to their skills. He encouraged the people to "keep their hands on the plow." He inspired people to believe that God would reward their diligent labor.

It is not difficult to recognize work that needs to be done. We are all good at seeing a problem and saying, "Somebody needs to do something about that." But usually nothing gets done until a Nehemiah comes along and says, "Let's tackle this job together." The most "Somebody" ever does is complain. Walls are never rebuilt until a Nehemiah shows up and challenges people to get organized and go to work. God's work usually requires a team effort.

We cannot overemphasize the fact that, inspired by Nehemiah, the people were willing to work. They "had a mind to work." I love that phrase, "a mind to work." What a blessing it is to see people step forward, get their hands dirty and get the job done!

Churches are made strong not by talk but by work. Talk is cheap. Most churches are filled with people who "yap" constantly about what the pastor and the staff ought to do. But call a "work day" and the talkers seldom show up. "We had to go out of town to see Aunt Sally," they whine.

Yet, thank God, the work goes on. Even a few people can get a lot done if they have the right perspective. The motive for which we work is crucial. We spoil it if we work for the applause of others or out of a desire to have "control." We work best when we offer our labor as an expression of gratitude for what the good Lord has done for us.

Attitude is so important. When we choose to be persistent in doing work for God, we must take care not to become mulish and inflexible. The Jews had to be flexible. Their enemies made it necessary for some of the Jews to stand guard while others worked. Henry Ward Beecher wisely observed, "The difference between perseverance and obstinacy is that one comes from a strong will, and the other from a strong won't."

We have not only the inspiring example of Nehemiah but also that of Jesus and the Apostle Paul. Jesus refused to let his enemies deter him from his mission. Resolutely he "set his face" toward Jerusalem so that he could do the work his Father had sent him to do. His willingness to "endure the cross, despising the shame," inspires us to persevere in our work when the going gets tough. And it always will.

When our burdens are heavy and we are tempted to quit, the words of Saint Paul can renew our determination, "Let us not grow weary in doing good, for at the proper time we will reap a harvest if we do not give up" (Galatians 6:9, NIV). How many times this scripture has caused me to cry out, "Lord, help me not to grow weary in doing what I believe is your will!" And He has always answered, "Alright I will; now get up and get back to work!"

In his day Winston Churchill's persistence changed the course of history for England. When the "walls" of England were being destroyed by Hitler's army, Churchill persuaded the English people to get organized, go to work and have faith in God. In response to Churchill's challenge, the people were willing to work, and with the help of God, they got the job done.

The virtue of persistence calls to mind Churchill's speech to students at Harrow, his old school, in 1941, when he said, "This is the lesson: never give in, never give in, never, never, never, never—in nothing, great or small, large or petty—never give in except to convictions of honor and good sense. Never yield to force; never yield to the apparently overwhelming might of the enemy." What a speech! What a difference the dogged spirit of Churchill made for his nation!

When we become weary in doing the work to which we have been called, crying will not help. Forget the tears. Stop feeling sorry for yourself and get back in the game with blood, sweat and persistence. Stay the course. Persevere. Then, when you think you have done all you can do, you will have the joy of realizing that unseen hands have helped you finish the job. +

30

Forgiveness can restore a broken relationship

In the *Dictionary of Quotations* only one person is quoted under the word "forgiveness." That person is Jesus and the quotation is the entire parable of the prodigal son found in the 15th chapter of the Gospel of Luke. Obviously the authors felt this statement on forgiveness has no equal. And they are correct.

While the story of the prodigal is one of literature's most compelling stories, Jesus had much more to say about forgiveness. The necessity of forgiveness was a cardinal teaching of Jesus. His teaching was penetratingly clear as in Matthew 6:14-15: *"For if you **forgive** men when they sin against you, your heavenly Father will also **forgive** you. But if you do not **forgive** men their sins, your Father will not **forgive** your sins"* (NIV).

Saint Paul continues this same theme in his letters to the young churches. Some of the apostle's most memorable teachings concern forgiveness. One of his priceless observations for me is Ephesians 4:32:

*"And be kind to one another, tenderhearted, **forgiving** one another, just as God in Christ **forgave** you." (NKJV)* That admonition to forgive has challenged me all my life. Even when I am slow to forgive, I know I must for the Lord leaves me no other alternative.

Paul learned firsthand the need for a forgiving spirit. Not everyone in the church at Corinth welcomed Paul's teaching. One man opposed Paul openly. For his offense he was disciplined by the church. In this Second Letter Paul encouraged the church to move on by forgiving the man and restoring him to the fellowship. Here Paul is practicing what Jesus preached. His sage words, "reaffirm your love for him," are worth remembering whenever we deal with conflict.

When a person has been grievously offended, forgiveness is never easy. It may become possible if we remember the grace of God. Paul shows us the crucial role of grace in forgiveness. Grace makes the impossible possible. God forgives us for our sins. He expects us to forgive those who sin against us. This we must do or our fellowship with the Father is broken. We cannot know God or love God and at the same time harbor resentment toward another person.

What can motivate us to repent of our resentment or hatred toward another? Paul's answer is "godly grief." Godly grief is grief that involves God. Godly grief makes us aware that we have sinned against God as well as the person we resent. Remember the cry of David as he repented of his adultery with Bathsheba? His was "godly" grief:

*"Have mercy on me, O God, according to your unfailing love; according to your great compassion blot out my transgressions. Wash away all my iniquity and cleanse me from my sin. For I know my transgressions, and my sin is always before me. **Against you, you only, have I sinned** and done what is evil **in your sight**. . . ." (Psalm 51:1-4, NIV)*

Godly grief can move us to genuine repentance. Paul commends the church for their repentance; it has brought him great joy. He hammers home the sharp contrast between godly grief and "worldly grief." Godly grief "produces a repentance that leads to salvation" while worldly grief "produces death." One leads to peace with God; the other to separation from God.

At one point Paul makes a beautiful request of his friends: "Make room in your hearts for us." Genuine Christianity is a matter of the heart. Despite our differences and inevitable conflict in the church, we can learn to open our hearts to one another! We can recognize that our sins grieve God and we can repent. We can forgive one another and allow grace to restore broken relationships. When we do this even pagans may testify, "Those Christians really do love one another!"

Satan has a field day when Christians engage in bitter conflict. He delights to see us focus on what is wrong with other people. He loves it when we think we are always right! But when we remember the Cross and repent of our own sins, we defeat Satan. He wants nothing to do

75

with genuine repentance, forgiveness and reconciliation.

Churches become stronger when Christians practice forgiveness. Old wounds can be healed by a forgiving spirit. Broken relationships can be mended by forgiveness. As the old gospel song puts it, "chords that were broken will vibrate once more," and joy will abound in the household of God! Great things can happen when we are willing to forgive those who have hurt us. +

31

When everything seems hopeless

Hopelessness is awful. It robs you of the desire to live and makes you wish you were dead. You feel like strong hands have you by the throat; you can hardly breathe. I know. I have struggled with this demon of the dark. Most of us have. Life is not a cake walk.

Job is the classic biblical example of one whose trials drove him into the pit of hopelessness. He was a man mired in the ash heap of miserable misfortune. When you read his story your heart breaks for the man. You can hardly fathom the depth of his anguish.

When we are down and out we like to think that our friends can help us. Job had friends but they were not much help. We can identify with the way Job felt about the counsel his friends gave him. Empty platitudes never assuage our pain. The shallow understanding of friends can sometimes feel like condemnation even when they are trying to help us.

Friends can make matters worse by admonishing us not to feel the way we feel. Real friends affirm us in our pain and give us a glimmer of hope that the night will not last forever. Job's friends drove him deeper into despair by insisting that he deserved his suffering. What Job needed, and what we all need, is someone who will help us cling to the idea that there is meaning in our madness.

A man named Elihu did help Job. He challenged him to question his assumptions about God. He helped Job affirm the greatness of God and reminded him that it is the nature of God to be just. So Job recants of having accused God of injustice. He eventually overcomes hopelessness and puts his full trust in God no matter what suffering he had to endure.

What helpful word can we say to our friends when the bottom

falls out? The best counsel may be this humorous maxim: "When you come to the end of your rope, tie a knot in it and hold on!" We could strengthen it by adding Jesus to the equation: "When you come to the end of your rope, trust Jesus; let him help you tie a knot in it and hold on!"

Essentially what we need is confidence in God's power to rescue us. The name "Jesus" means "God to the rescue." The strange paradox is that by refusing to rescue Jesus from death on the cross, God made it possible for us to be rescued from the kingdom of darkness.

When all seems hopeless we can remember the cross. The cross represents utter hopelessness. Yet God took over and turned the cross into a symbol of hope. He was able to transform defeat into victory and despair into hope. The empty cross reminds us of the resurrection and the Christian hope that death is not the end.

The idea of tying a knot in a rope may seem foolish. If I tie a knot in my rope I am still at the end of it. I am still helpless unless someone rescues me. This is where trust comes in.

To trust God is not only to hold on but also to ask him to hold your hand. We trust God by hearing him say to us what he said to Isaiah, "For I, the Lord your God, will hold your right hand, saying to you, 'Fear not, I will help you'" (Isaiah 41:13). Ultimately faith is believing that I can hold on to the rope because God is holding on to me. To hold on is to trust God's timetable. When we are in a jam we want God to come immediately. Though he can he seldom does. He waits for us to realize that we cannot save ourselves, that he is our only hope. Then he comes in the moment he has chosen to deliver us. He leaves us no "wiggle room" to suppose we have saved ourselves; he shows us that we are saved by grace and grace alone.

The Psalmist shows us how to overcome despair: "Why are you downcast, O my soul? Why so disturbed within me? Put your hope in God, for I will yet praise Him, my Savior and my God" (Psalm 42:11, NIV)

Our greatest advantage is the cross. The Romans on that fateful day looked at Jesus hanging on that cruel cross and assumed that was the end of him. But they were wrong. They had no way of knowing that

God was using the cross to offer reconciliation to the human race. If one day all seems hopeless remember that you can ask Jesus to help you tie a knot in your rope and hold on. He will come. I have bet my life on it! Until he does, hold on! That is the best way to overcome hopelessness. +

32

When you feel like giving up

Life is hard. There are times when evil wins. We do the right thing but wrong prevails. Those who lie and cheat have the upper hand. We see a tiny light in the tunnel of our darkness but it turns out to be a train that runs over us.

In such times we are tempted to throw up our hands and quit. Why keep trying to do the right thing if we lose? Doubt takes over and we wonder if the way of love really is the winning way. When our faith is tested by the difficulties of life, it helps to remember that God was not surprised. Nothing surprises God. He knows what is coming. Reading the Bible reinforces this truth. God uses the Bible to strengthen my faith.

One way he does that is by inspiring me when I read about people like the prophet Daniel. Reading the story of Daniel reminds me that God will help me if I turn to him. I don't understand everything I read in the Book of Daniel but I still find great lessons in this small book. Take, for example, that story about the king's dream. The king's demand of Daniel and the wise men was impossible. He ordered them to tell him what he had dreamed and what his dream meant. The wise men gave up. It was impossible to know what the king had dreamed.

Daniel, however, turned to the Lord in prayer. He did not turn to his own cleverness; he turned to God. God answered Daniel's prayer so Daniel could tell the king both his dream and its meaning. The challenge for us is to believe that God will help us like he helped Daniel. When there seems to be no human solution, we can by faith turn to God. The world says, "Give up." Faith says, "Turn to God."

Daniel believed what Jesus would teach us years later – "Nothing is impossible with God!" We can learn to ask God, and trust God, even when our situation seems hopeless. No matter what the problem, God is able to help us.

Our friends in Zambia, Alfred and Muumbe Kalembo, had a problem. Their neighbors begged them to teach their small children to read and write. The only space available was a small room that served as Alfred's study.

"If God wants us to have a school, he is able to make it happen," the Kalembos said. So they decided to turn the little room into a school, naming the school the "God Is Able School for Children." Soon Alfred's study became a classroom where Muumbe would teach ten children. Realizing they could enroll a hundred more children if they had the facilities, Alfred and Muumbe believed what Daniel believed – God is able! Today they are operating three schools and building a fourth!

My friend John has been successful in business more than once. In fact, three times he lost everything and had to start over from scratch. But he refused to give up. While he lost everything financially, he did not lose his faith. He continued to believe that God was able to help him succeed – and he has! A sign in a churchyard expresses what John believes: "When you have nothing but God, you have everything you need."

Many people have everything but God and they are miserable. What they fail to see is that what they cannot see is what really matters. Things have no eternal value. The Bible teaches us that what is visible has no lasting meaning; only the invisible lasts forever!

A man in Alabama become so successful that he was considered the state's most generous philanthropist. He had homes in several states. He had his own private jet. Then his world collapsed. He was fired as CEO of the very company he had built. His success was achieved, his accusers say, through fraud and deception. His "kingdom" of wealth and extravagance crumbled, like a sand castle.

Daniel was not impressed with earthly kingdoms. They have no future. God, however, according to Daniel, is building a kingdom "that shall never be destroyed."

We may lose "the greatest job in the world." We may lose our dream home. Our worldly treasures may vanish into thin air. But what we have invested in the Kingdom of God we cannot lose. What we have given away, in the service of Jesus, will be ours forever.

When the world's kingdoms are tottering and falling all around us, we can rejoice that we belong to an eternal Kingdom, the Kingdom that will remain when everything else has been destroyed.

Think about Daniel. We do not know if he wore expensive clothes, if he lived in a fine home or if he drove an expensive camel. We do not know if he was a member of a Country Club or if he was privileged to dine in "The Club" of his city. What we do know about Daniel is that he believed God was able to meet his needs and that God's kingdom could never be destroyed.

Should it not be our fervent prayer that we may live with such faith in these days? God is able! To believe that, and to live by it, could be the key to great living until our journey ends. +

33

Learning to serve others

As a child Betsy had a heart for God. Her eyes sparkled when the conversation was about living for Jesus. Her parents, devout disciples of Jesus and faithful leaders in their church, encouraged her to trust God. In her teen years Betsy shared with me her desire to live as a servant of Jesus Christ. She had noticed that I always added the letters, "SJC," to my name when signing letters. She wanted to know why I did it.

I told her my story of receiving a letter from Estelle Carver when I was a young preacher. I met Estelle in a retreat. She impacted my life in a powerful way. She was an English teacher but a devout Christian and a brilliant witness for Christ. Estelle was a friend of the evangelist E. Stanley Jones. He invited her to teach a Bible study in many of his retreats.

Ms. Carver signed her letter "Estelle, sjc." The next time I saw her, I asked her what the initials meant; she said simply, "Servant of Jesus Christ." As she shared this with me, I knew instantly that I would sign my name in the same way for the rest of my life. And I have – for more than 50 years.

At first I felt embarrassed about doing it. For a while I had to actually force myself to continue doing it. I feared my friends might think I was doing it for "show." They will think me a fool.

But I overcame my fears and steadfastly signed my name, "Walter, sjc." Now it flows easily as though it is part of my name. Early on I did it primarily to remind myself of my true identity. So it has been more for my benefit than for the readers of my letters. It has constantly reminded me that this is my sole reason to exist – to live in the world as a servant of Jesus Christ. Nothing else matters more.

Elton Trueblood called Mark 10:45 the most revolutionary verse in the Bible. It is a statement by Jesus about himself: "For even the Son of Man did not come to be served, but to serve, and to give his life as a ransom for many." His words have humbled me often as I have struggled with the common temptation to have others serve me rather than live as a servant to others. To choose to live as a servant of others is indeed a revolutionary idea.

Rulers in the first century (as in our own time) had their servants. They expected others to serve them. Power and wealth meant the privilege of having servants. Jesus, however, turned this idea upside down. Though he was the Son of God, Jesus insisted that he had not come to be served but to serve and to give his life for others.

Jesus saw himself as a servant of others. He called upon his disciples to follow his example: become servants of others. "Wash feet as I have washed your feet," Jesus said. Servanthood, then, is the unmistakable key to Christian living.

We may observe that Jesus did not rebuke his disciples for wanting to become "great," as though desiring greatness is somehow evil. He simply reminded them that the pathway to greatness – in the eyes of God – is not in power, fame or fortune but in serving others.

Serving others is not glamorous. It sometimes involves doing menial tasks that "servants" usually handle. Pride, the monster that seeks to destroy us all, can cause us to think we are "too important" for servant work. Such work is "beneath" us.

Yet when I think of true servants of Jesus I think of a man like Robert. He was never president of a bank or mayor of the town. He never served as a trustee or a leader of his church. He was simply available when someone needed help. He would drive someone to see a doctor, take a hot meal to a sick person or visit a lonely home-bound person. Robert did those things not for pay or vain glory but because he was a servant of Jesus Christ.

Speaking of servants, Betsy, the girl I mentioned earlier, is now in her thirties. She took up the habit of signing her name "Betsy, sjc" when she was a teenager. But even more important she has followed her dream to live as a servant of Jesus Christ. She does that by serving poor children in Mozambique, Haiti or wherever Samaritan's Purse ministry sends her.

The bottom line of all this: If you want to live a great life then find a way to serve others. While it is not an easy choice, servanthood is the key to living a life that matters. +

34

God can use our suffering

Victory over suffering begins with the conviction that God can redeem and use our suffering. Many biblical stories highlight this truth. One of the best is the account of Joseph's suffering found in Genesis, the first book of the Bible.

God redeemed and made sense of Joseph's suffering. But God did even more. He also redeemed the suffering of Joseph's brothers and that of their father Jacob.

Joseph's brothers suffered for more than 20 long years the guilt of getting rid of their arrogant brother. Every time they saw a pit of any kind, they must have relived the sight of their helpless brother Joseph in the pit where they had thrown him.

The brothers had done an evil thing – and they had gotten away with it. No CSI team turned up evidence to expose their wickedness. For years they must have been nervous when strangers came by their home; perhaps they had come to inform Jacob of their evil deed.

Their sleep must have been interrupted countless nights. They would wake up in a cold sweat, having heard in their dreams Joseph begging them not to leave him to die in the pit. Guilt has a way of torturing us relentlessly for our sins.

The sight of any young boy wearing a coat of many colors would have triggered their guilt. Instantly they would see the anguish on the face of their brother Joseph the last time they saw him. How they must have hated the sight of any man wearing such a jacket.

When at last Joseph revealed his identity as their brother, the brothers' load of guilt turned instantly into fear. They thought, "We are dead men now; our brother will take his revenge and kill us."

To their amazement they found that revenge was not on Joseph's mind. Instead he offered them forgiveness, inviting them to see what Joseph saw – the gracious hand of God at work, using their treacherous deed as a means of blessing them and many others. Instead of justice, Joseph's brothers experienced the kindness of God.

The heavy weight of their guilt was removed, like a burden rolled away by the power of God. Not only would their hungry families have food to eat in years of famine, they were savoring as well the sweet taste of forgiveness. After so many years of suffering for their sin, God had redeemed their suffering!

How Jacob must have suffered over the years, remembering the son he had loved so dearly and mourning his tragic death. The death of a child takes something out of a father. It is like a chunk of his heart being torn out. He never gets over it though he manages somehow to go on with life. But life is never the same. The heart-wrenching loss of one's own flesh and blood colors life with somber shades of realism.

Finally, after many long years of heartache, Jacob discovers that his beloved son Joseph was not killed by wild animals. He is alive! And Joseph is now in a position to provide for his entire family and spare them from years of famine. Though Jacob must pack up and move once again, he will now be blessed by the reunion of his family and their rescue from poverty.

All of this, Jacob realizes, has occurred because God had a plan to use Joseph for the benefit of his entire family. God has redeemed Jacob's suffering by turning his sorrow into joy.

And what of Joseph's suffering? His tears flowed for much more than the emotional reunion with his brothers. Incredible joy swept his soul as it dawned on him that God had a purpose for all Joseph's suffering. Suddenly God showed him that everything had happened for a reason. It was not his brothers who had sent him to Egypt; God had put him there! And God was now using Joseph "to preserve a remnant and to keep many survivors alive."

Joseph saw the purpose of his life as he gazed at his frightened brothers. He realized the futility of revenge. He understood the beauty of forgiveness. He saw God at work. He knew the unbelievable joy of knowing that God was using his life to bless others. There is no greater joy!

Believe that a merciful God can redeem and use your suffering and you are on the way to victory! +

35

Listening with the ears of the heart

People use different techniques to get attention. The famous words of Shakespeare come to mind: "Friends, Romans, countrymen, lend me your ears."

A presiding officer at a head table may tap on a glass or clap his hands to get attention. A football coach may say to his players during a scrimmage, "Listen up!"

A frustrated wife may speak sharply to the husband who has buried himself in a newspaper, "You have not heard a word I have said; will you put that paper down and listen to me?"

Jesus used subtle humor to get the attention of his audience. On one occasion when speaking to a crowd about John the Baptist, Jesus said, "He who has ears, let him hear." People surely smiled. Everyone has ears.

But not everyone "uses" their ears. Some people do not listen. We explain that by saying that the words of the speaker "went in one ear and out the other." That happens to all of us unless we pay careful attention to the person speaking.

Jesus was simply reminding his listeners that they must be intentional about listening in order to comprehend what they hear. Earlier translations of this phrase used by Jesus are not as clear as recent ones. The King James, for example, has Jesus say, "Who hath ears to hear, let him hear."

Goodspeed improved on it: "Let him who has ears listen!" The NRSV improved on Goodspeed: "Let anyone with ears listen!" The Living Bible Translation offers the clearest version yet: "Anyone who is willing to hear should listen and understand!"

The implication of Jesus is that listening should lead to under-standing and understanding to action. Hearing must be translated into deeds. Understanding must result in obedience. To listen and understand, and fail to act in obedience, is not to have heard at all.

Jesus' reference to ears was his way of saying, "Hey, listen up now, this is important!" In a similar way a writer may use a bold font for a word or end a sentence with an exclamation point (or a "squealer").

The phrase about listening reappears in the Book of Revelation when Christ speaks to the seven churches: "Anyone who is willing to hear should listen to the Spirit and understand what the Spirit is say-ing to the churches" (Living Bible). This reinforces the idea that the risen Christ in John's Revelation is the same Christ who spoke in the parables recorded in the Gospels.

The importance of listening is stressed in the biblical story of Jesus on the Mount of Transfiguration. There Moses and Elijah ap-peared with Jesus to confirm his role as the Messiah. Jesus' counte-nance was transfigured with divine glory. But observe what God said: "This is my beloved Son; listen to him."

Jesus urged the people and the disciples to listen to what he said and God commands us to listen to Jesus. And listening to Jesus must be important because the Bible says he is the "Word" of God made flesh! An old hymn, "How Firm a Foundation," raises the ultimate question: "What more can he say?"

Hearing an internal voice is, of course, never easy. A multitude of other "voices" are clamoring for our attention. None of us ever re-ally "hears" Jesus until we intentionally shut out other noises and give him a chance to be heard in the silence of our souls.

Many things can become like wax in our ears which makes us deaf to the voice of Jesus. We can become too busy to listen to God. We can get so focused on the body that we have no time for the soul. We may even become obstinate and like a child put our fingers in our ears to keep from hearing what Jesus is saying to us. A friend of mine refuses to go to church for fear God will speak to him.

The danger in refusing to listen is that we may eventually lose the capacity to hear the one voice to which we should pay attention.

When the ears become atrophied, the soul is not far behind.

At the last, when God draws the curtain upon the stage of time, it is certain that we will hear his voice. There will be no wax in our ears then. Either we will hear him say, "Depart from me, I never knew you;" or we will hear him say, "Welcome home, good and faithful servant."

When Jesus walked the dusty roads of Nazareth his disciples were "hard of hearing." We are much like them. Eventually, however, those first century disciples listened and understood Jesus with the ears of their hearts. Then they acted in obedience and the Jesus Movement spread throughout the world.

If you will pause now and listen closely, really listen, you may hear his quiet inner voice say again, "Let anyone with ears listen!" But you can only hear him by listening with the ears of your heart. +

36

Authentic Christians are servants

My friend Fred Fuller died in 2014. Fred was a gentle giant, a gracious servant of Christ and a fellow United Methodist preacher.

I discovered at Fred's funeral that a little known verse in the New Testament was precious to him. The verse is First Corinthians 4:1 – "Think of us in this way, as servants of Christ and stewards of God's mysteries."

Fred wanted people to think of the clergy as servants of Christ. But it was more than an idea with Fred. It was a conviction that he practiced. He spent his life serving others. The people who knew him well recognized Fred as an authentic servant of Christ.

Fred took his cue from the Apostle Paul who wrote that verse to the Corinthian Christians. Paul described himself as a servant of Christ and a steward of God. He spent his life making Christ known and inviting people to embrace Christ as Lord. His will was subservient to the will of Christ.

Like his Lord Jesus, Paul's first concern was the Kingdom of God, not the Kingdom of Paul. He never asked for a dime to erect anything that would perpetuate his own name. On the contrary he did everything within his power to make known the name of his Savior.

Paul promoted servanthood and he practiced it. Jesus was his Boss, his Lord, from whom he received his marching orders. Paul's response to the Great Commission of Jesus was the greatest response made by any person in the first century. For Paul nothing was more important than to take up the cross and "go make disciples of all nations" – even if it cost him his life. And it did.

In recent years the word "servant" has been glamorized. We have added the word "leader" to it; we want to be known as "servant leaders" of the church. This distinction tempts us to feel more important than the common people. We crave recognition and praise for our hard work. Some have even quit the church because they did not receive the recognition they thought they deserved.

Older translations of the Bible show that Paul used the word "slave" instead of servant. He identified himself simply as a "slave of Christ." In choosing the word "slave" Paul showed us his heart. He thought it a high privilege to serve as a slave of Jesus Christ. He was willing to surrender entirely to the mastery of Christ. Christ was everything; Paul was content to be Christ's slave and to do what he was told to do. After all, to Paul Christ was the visible expression of the invisible God, the One before whom "every knee will bow" one day.

We who serve Christ today are prone to think of ourselves "more highly than we ought to think" – to borrow a phrase from Paul. Some of us may even imagine that Christ should be proud to have us on his team, as gifted as we are. But this is not a new problem. It was the problem Paul addressed when he spoke of being "puffed up in favor of one against another." We get puffed up when we compare ourselves with others. Slaves, on the other hand, are less likely to become puffed up about anything.

Instead of foolishly comparing ourselves to others, and stimulating resentment in the fellowship, we should remember our calling – to live as servants and stewards under the Lordship of Christ. Stewards are expected to be trustworthy, to care well for the responsibilities we are given. What we have is not actually ours but a gift on loan from God. He expects us to be faithful stewards, serving responsibly with gratitude for the mercy he has shown us.

Puffed up people have a gift for dodging true servanthood. They want control so they can have their way. They desire power more than an opportunity to serve. They want to tell other Christians what to do rather that bowing to the will of Christ. This attitude weakens the witness of the church.

Mother Teresa showed us how to be a slave of Christ. After receiving the Nobel Prize for Peace, she declined many other invitations to be wined and dined and honored for her work with the poor. She realized that her service to the dying was more important than attending banquets to be recognized for her achievements. She thanked the people who sought to honor her but remained at her post so she could help the poor and dying know they were loved.

Harry Denman was a slave of Christ and desired no other image. When he retired from serving as head of evangelism for the Methodist Church, his friends held a great reception in his honor. Several hundred people were present and enjoyed delicious food and drink. Harry was not there. He was miles away preaching about his friend Jesus in a little country church.

People like Fred Fuller model for us what it means to serve as a faithful steward and humble servant of Christ. With God's help we can model that kind of winsome discipleship for others. At least we can try. It all begins with a willingness to think of ourselves as servants and stewards of Jesus Christ. Paul did. Fred did. We can too. +

37

Get up every day and try to do what's right

Pastors often counsel people who have gotten in trouble by doing the wrong thing. I invite people to have hope. Though the past cannot be undone, a new beginning is possible. My advice: Bury the past in the sea of God's forgiveness and get up every morning determined to do the right thing in every situation.

A new beginning may require a change in the company you keep. If you run with losers you will likely become a loser. Winners associate with good people, people who are doing the right thing. People who are doing the wrong thing pull you down. People who respect neither the laws of God nor man will persuade you to make wrong decisions. Running with the wrong crowd invites disaster.

There are evil people everywhere but there are also many good people, godly people. They are not hard to find. They are the people who consistently do the right thing. They treat others fairly. They refuse to lie or cheat to make a profit. They are not perfect. But they simply get up every morning and try to do what is right.

Such people are often Christians or Jews. Both Jews and Christians take their cue from God as to what is right and wrong. That is why they are called "godly" people. Ask them to explain "good" and Jews and Christians may sometimes mention the words of an Old Testament prophet named Micah. His definition of what is good is one of the most beloved verses in the Bible, Micah 6:8:

He has told you, O mortal, what is good; and what does the Lord require of you but to do justice, and to love kindness, and to walk humbly with your God?

Micah summed up brilliantly what God expects of his children

– to practice justice, kindness and humility. He warned us that God is not impressed with our "offerings" if at the same time we are mistreating people and proudly "strutting our stuff" in God's face.

Observe that Micah uses the word "requires," not requests. Fairness, mercy and humility are not suggested but expected. The consequences of not measuring up to God's expectations are severe, according to Micah. Refuse to do what is right and God will not answer you when you cry out to him. He will "hide his face."

Godly people try to live by biblical standards. They believe the Bible shows them how God wants them to live. Godly folks do the right thing because they are children of God and doing the right thing "runs in the family."

My dad was a godly man. Not in words but in deeds. He got up every day determined to do what was right. As a young pastor godly people got my attention. Frank Hugh Pierce was such a man. He ran a body shop and raised a family on a modest income. He did not have much of this world's goods but he did have integrity. He refused to bilk insurance companies for repairs he had not made. Day after day he found the moral courage to do the right thing.

The highest standard by which Christians measure their lives is the example of Jesus Christ. Jesus is God's eternal "Plumb Line." Conduct not "in line" with the character of Jesus is conduct that is "out of plumb" with the will of God. And Jesus made it clear that the people who are going to heaven are those who do the will of God.

Being accountable to a few basically good people is a good way to find the backbone to do the right thing. Over the years I have found it a blessing to meet regularly with a few other men who helped me stay on the straight and narrow path.

Looking for a way to get out of trouble and make a new start? There is no better way than to get up every morning and try to do the right thing. Sooner or later, with God's help, you'll be a winner. +

38

Things worth doing as long as you live

Over the course of a normal lifetime each of us has the opportunity to do many things. Some bring us joy, others disappointment. Ultimately we discover that there is not enough time or money to do everything. So we make choices and do what we can while time and energy are available.

As we grow older we must contend with a dwindling supply of strength and enthusiasm. We tire more easily. We are more vulnerable to cynicism. We can more easily get down on ourselves and others than when we were younger. The aging process takes its toll on the best of us.

There is, however, value in remembering that there are certain things which are worth doing as long as we live. These things we must not neglect lest we lose our zest for living. Let us think together about the things that are worth doing as long as we have breath. Make your own list and compare it to mine.

One, encourage others. The value of encouragement cannot be overestimated. Everybody needs it. Everybody can give it. Every situation is improved by the presence of encouragement. Nobody lives well without it. Children need it. Young people need it. Young adults need it. Old people must have it to survive. Look around you every day and encourage everyone you meet. Offer it even when people seemed shocked and surprised by it.

Two, speak to people in a friendly way. Many people in our society feel no need to speak to others. Sales clerks in our stores sometimes simply tell the customer the cost of an item and extend a hand for the money. Then they return the change without offering even so much as a "thank you" for shopping in the store. But both customer and clerk will feel better if they take a moment to offer a kind, friendly word to each other. The challenge, of course, is to speak graciously to someone even when they refuse to respond in kind.

Three, smile at people. Offer people a smile even when you are hurting yourself. Usually you will get a smile in return. I smile a lot because I don't want even a stranger passing me to say, "There goes old sourpuss; he must have indigestion." We have a choice when we meet people. We can frown, stare indifferently, or smile. A friendly smile can sometimes make a person's day.

Four, keep a positive attitude even when others are being negative. Look for something positive in every situation. Negative thinking never helps anyone. You will never go home at night, put your head on your pillow, and say, "What a great blessing all that negative thinking was to me today!" But positive thinking can inspire people to believe in themselves and make the most of a difficult experience.

Five, be thankful for your friends and let them know you care. A good friend is more precious than silver or gold. We are wise to value and cultivate our friendships. True friends help us to admit the truth about ourselves and encourage us to do our best in the daily tests of life. Real friendship can exist only when there is both giving and taking; it does not last where there is no mutual helpfulness. When our friends are hurting, we can hardly sleep at night. That's because we love them and we want the best for them. It hurts to see our friends hurt. We can afford to lose our possessions; we cannot afford to lose our friends. When that happens, life becomes sour and meaningless.

Six, do something thoughtful and loving for someone in need. If an apple a day is helpful, a good deed at day is more helpful. A good deed can be simple and inexpensive. Send someone a note or a card, or perhaps a letter. Share your turnip greens with someone. Mow someone's lawn. Give someone who is sick or discouraged a good book like *The Prayer of Jabez* by Bruce Wilkinson, or *Balcony People* by Joyce Heatherly. Love can be expressed in many small and wonderful ways.

Seven, praise God for your blessings. Enjoy what you have and be satisfied with it. Refuse to wish you could trade places with your neighbor. Contentment is its own reward. Consider yourself blessed, for you are. Millions of people are worse off than you are. Thank God even for your aches and pains for they remind you that you are alive, and life itself is a precious gift. Refuse to join the chorus of this world's complainers who see nothing but the dark side. In spite of all that is mean, evil, and ugly, God is still good and he remains willing to bless those who trust him.

We cannot do everything but these are a few things that are worth doing as long as we have breath. And while none of us can do these things perfectly, we should be ashamed to die without having tried. +

39

Forgive so you can live

There are few more beautiful stories of reconciliation than the biblical account of Jacob and Esau. These words paint an unforgettable picture of the power of forgiveness: *"Esau ran to meet him, and embraced him, and fell on his neck and kissed him, and they wept"* (Genesis 33:4).

Two brothers, estranged for more than 20 years, fall into each other's arms. Tears stream down their cheeks as they offer each other forgiveness. The chains of hatred, guilt, fear and resentment are broken. The burden of their separation rolls away. Their hearts pound with joy. The war between them is over. They are reconciled!

The fear belonged to Jacob. Imagine what fear possessed him when he saw coming with his brother Esau 400 armed men! Jacob knew his brother had promised to kill him. He must have thought, "Now Esau is coming to keep his promise! I am a dead man!"

True to his nature Jacob began scrambling to find a way out of his dilemma. Always the schemer Jacob figures Esau will not attack him as long as he is surrounded by women and children. Fear for his life drove him to bow to the ground seven times in the hope that his brother would have mercy on him.

Then, to Jacob's complete surprise, Esau offers him reconciling love instead of a sword. They embrace, kiss and weep. The pain of the past is forgotten. Yet Jacob still wonders about his own safety for he refers to himself as "your servant" and addresses Esau as "my lord." Hoping to win Esau's favor, Jacob offers gifts to his brother.

This beautiful story is similar to two scenes in the New Testament. One is the story of the Prodigal Son told by Jesus in Luke 15. Esau's running to embrace his brother is strikingly similar to what the forgiving father does when he sees the prodigal coming home: "But while he was still a long way off, his father saw him and was filled with compassion for him; he ran to his son, threw his arms around him and kissed him."

The other scene is that in Acts where Ananias casts his fear aside and placing his hands on the blind and helpless Saul, speaks to him as his brother (chapter 9). Jesus helped Ananias to realize that he and Saul were no longer enemies but brothers.

These stories give us a window into the nature of God. From the beginning God has helped men who had become enemies to be reconciled in order to live together as brothers.

Though Jacob may have been a deceitful man he could still recognize grace when he saw it. Esau must have blushed when Jacob said to him, *"truly to see your face is like seeing the face of God – since you have received me with such favor."*

There is no reason to suspect that Jacob's words were flattery. He is obviously sincere, deeply overwhelmed by the forgiving love offered him by his brother. He had expected the swift hand of justice. He received the gracious hand of mercy.

Centuries later forgiveness was a central theme in the teaching of Jesus. He made it clear that to receive God's forgiveness for our sins we must be willing to forgive others for their sins against us. We cannot live as citizens of the kingdom of God without practicing forgiveness.

Forgiveness is the very heart of the gospel. Jesus died so that through the shedding of his blood our sins could be forgiven. At the last supper he took the cup and said, *"This is the cup of the new agreement, the new covenant in my blood which is shed for many for the forgiveness of sins."*

E. Stanley Jones helped me to see how necessary forgiveness is if we are to live healthy lives. To refuse to forgive those who hurt us is to ruin our own health. Many of us are "sick" with various ailments because we have chosen to hate rather than forgive someone.

Brother Stanley told the story of a man who worked for the railroad in India. The man's job took him away from home and his wife for long periods of time. On one of those trips he gave in to sexual temptation and took a mistress. Over time his guilt about this relationship grew in his heart until finally it became unbearable.

One day while he was home he called his wife into the room and began to pour out the sordid story of his sin against her and their marriage vows. Jones said the man's wife turned as pale as death. She staggered back and leaned against the wall and then great tears trickled down her face. As he continued to confess his sin, she looked as if she had been beaten by a whip.

What the man's confession did to his wife profoundly affected him. At the time he professed to be a Christian but the pain he caused his wife moved him to genuine faith in Christ. He said, "In that moment, seeing her there in that state, I saw the meaning of the cross. I saw love crucified by a sin, my sin. I could see Christ on the cross crucified by my sin, even as I was crucifying my wife." His wife's forgiveness helped him become a new man in Christ. Her forgiving love made possible a new relationship and a stronger marriage.

Hatred creates hell for the hater. Forgiveness creates the joy that Jesus said erupts in heaven "over one sinner who repents." As we travel the journey of life, we are all hurt by others not once but many times. In our pain we have a choice. We can hate or we can forgive.

Forgiveness opens the door to reconciliation, freedom and new life. Esau and Jacob made the right choice. We have an advantage those two men did not have. We have, if we will but listen, the living Christ whispering in our ear, "Your sins are forgiven. I nailed them to the Cross. Now stop hating and forgive so you can live!" That we must do if we are to become truly alive. Otherwise, though we may be breathing, we will remain dead in our sins. And dead is no way to live!

+

40

Wandering in the wilderness

I lost a good friend on Christmas day, 2013. Jay Andrews was only 54. His sudden and unexpected death was a jarring reminder to live each day to the full since we know not what a day will bring forth.

I met Jay at an altar many years ago. We prayed together and became friends. Decades later I had the privilege of serving on staff with him at our church. He had a good mind and a big heart. No day with Jay was without laughter because he was forever bubbling over with joyous enthusiasm. He was a fun person to be around.

Jay had a pastor's heart. His great longing was to serve God as a pastor. A few years back he called to share the good news that he had been appointed pastor of Snowdoun United Methodist Church south of Montgomery. Though the church was struggling Jay was convinced he could help the people revitalize the church – and he did.

The reason for Jay's success as a pastor is no secret. He loved the people and they loved him. He called his church family "friends beyond compare, rays of light in an often-dark world." God has a way of using pastors who think like that.

Jay wrote a good book three years ago. I have read it three or four times, twice since Jay's death. The book 's title is **Wanderings in the Wilderness**, with the subtitle **The Journey Back to Eden**, published by WestBow Press, a division of Thomas Nelson. It is available from most bookstores and from Amazon.

Like most of us Jay knew about wandering in the wilderness. But he found his way out and he spent the best part of his life showing people how to stop such aimless wandering. Jay gave up rambling in the dark and began enjoying what he called "the glory of the journey to the Promised Land."

I want to give you a taste of Jay's gifted writing. He uses his vivid imagination to describe the wandering experiences of several biblical characters. I love the way he pictures Paul and Silas in that hell-hole called a jail. Overwhelmed by the stench of death, Paul is angry and frustrated. So Jay writes:

"Each time he moved, the burning of torn flesh reminded him of the angry faces of the men who beat them. Open wounds on the cold stone of a damp wall had killed many a prisoner as infection took its toll. A chill ran up his spine as he felt something crawl over his foot. Chains rattled and shackles tore deeper into his ankles as he kicked away the unwelcome intruder. His legs were stiff; he could not raise one arm; his head felt swollen; and he was dizzy. His belly burned with hunger as he heard the laughter of the guards above....

"His heart felt defeat. He thought he had been called to Macedonia by a vision, but maybe not. This is not what he expected....Perhaps he had misinterpreted his calling....It was too much to bear. The Lord had finally asked too much of him. Quietly he wept. He could not go on any more.

"'Brother Paul,' a weak, raspy voice whispered.

"He could not be sure, but, between the coughs, it sounded like Silas.

"'Are ...you awake? Perhaps...maybe...we could...pray; perhaps the Lord would have pity on us.

"As Paul began to pray, Silas began to sing softly and gently.

"Paul's voice grew in strength.

"An eerie silence fell on the inner cell. The whimpering stopped.

"The cries of agony grew silent.

"The pain had ceased.

"Silas sang louder and Paul joined his melody of praise. A few prisoners joined in; the others, too weak to sing, just listened and enjoyed the peace of the moment.

"The distant rumble was felt before it was heard, and soon light flooded the once dark prison and the captive's shackles fell to the floor...."

I will stop there in the hope that Jay's words have whetted your appetite for more. Believe me, this is a good book by a man who became a good guide for people who were weary of wandering in the wilderness. +

41

People can change

If you are tempted to give up on someone, give me five minutes of your time. That's how long it will take me to tell you a Bible story that could influence your decision.

Bible stories are about real people, not cartoon characters like Batman and Robin. Throughout its pages the Bible portrays people just like us, people who make a mess of their lives. But the golden thread in the Bible is about a God who keeps giving losers a second chance.

The story I want you to consider is found in Genesis. It is about a father and his sons. Jacob, the father, is no hero. He makes one poor decision after another. His sons follow his example. Except for the youngest whose name is Joseph. But early on even Joseph, who eventually becomes a Super Hero, is a young whippersnapper, a spoiled brat and an arrogant tattletale. In fairness to Joseph, however, we must credit Jacob for Joseph's arrogance. Jacob let it be known that Joseph, Rachel's firstborn, was his favorite son. He showed his favoritism by giving Joseph a colorful robe that set him apart from his brothers. The robe made Joseph proud. He strutted around in his nice robe, talking about his dreams, while his older brothers did the hard work of tending the sheep. They began to hate Joseph. When he told his brothers about his dreams they hated him even more.

Jacob's favoritism stirred up jealousy in the hearts of Joseph's brothers. A wise father would have known that playing favorites with his children can lead to disastrous consequences. Jealousy often turns into hatred. Hatred can lead to murder. Marriages and families are often destroyed by jealousy.

Joseph's dream talk did not bother his brothers as much as his interpretation of his dreams. That God spoke to people through dreams was a popular belief back then. What irritated Joseph's brothers was that Joseph portrayed himself as the Big Cheese in his dreams with his brothers bowing humbly before him. Little wonder that his eleven brothers reacted angrily.

Their anger only increased when Joseph went on to tell them of another dream. In this one Joseph saw his parents, Jacob and Rachel, as well as all eleven of his brothers bowing down to him. That was the straw that broke the camel's back for his brothers. Enough is enough! They were ready now to entertain the idea of killing their brother. Their hatred had reached the boiling point.

The brothers' plan to kill Joseph was thwarted at the last minute by his brother Reuben. He convinced his brothers to leave Joseph in a pit to die rather than kill him. Joseph's life was preserved so that he could be sold to Ishmaelite traders who took him to Egypt.

The real hero of this story is God. Jacob, Joseph, and his brothers win no merit badges for their behavior. They remind us of ourselves and the way we also screw up our lives with poor decisions.

A pastor friend confessed to me that he was about ready to quit the ministry. He was discouraged by his own failures and the moral failures of some of his own children. I told him I understood because I had sometimes had those same feelings.

But I reminded him that, even if he was ready to give up on God, God was not going to give up on him. I told him that the only people God can turn to are folks just like him and me – folks who have a gift for screwing things up. There are no perfect, righteous warriors to whom God can turn for service.

This is why I wanted you to listen to the story of Jacob and his boys. God does not give up on us because we make poor decisions. Jacob made his share. Joseph made his. Joseph's brothers made theirs. But through it all God was at work. God had a plan for all those men, not merely Joseph. God used each one to accomplish his will and he did so despite their imperfections and foolish choices.

Eventually all the men in that Bible story made decisions to honor God. So the bottom line is this: People can change. Grace makes that possible. This gives us hope for our own lives. If we will hang in with God, he will hang in with us. Along the way, if we make ourselves available to him,

God will give us the grace to forgive ourselves, accept his forgiveness and start making better choices.

Jacob did. Joseph did. His brothers did. We can too, by the grace of God. And one day he will welcome us home to the place where imperfect children may spend eternity being perfected by the loving Father who never gives up on his own. Glory! Just thinking about such a God makes me want to sing, "Lord, I want to be in that number, when the saints go marching in!"

Winston Churchill made famous the phrase, "Never give up!" Think about that when you are tempted to give up on someone who has made pitiful decisions. God never gives up on us. And with his help you can refuse to give up on someone who needs your compassion. You could twist Sir Winston's phrase a bit and say it this way: I will never give up on a person who has made poor decisions because people can change. +

42

The astounding claims of Jesus

Imagine one of your neighbors saying to you, "I am the bread of life."
You would probably figure he had had a stroke. And you might reply,
"Yeah, right. Well, see you later" as you walked away.

Yet you would admit upon reflection that we all have hungers of
the heart that cornbread and biscuits cannot satisfy. We need some
kind of "spiritual" bread that will nourish the soul.

Even some atheists acknowledge this need. Though a professed
atheist, novelist Marghanita Laski wrote mostly about religion. Not
long before she died Laski said to a Christian friend, "I envy you Christians; you have someone to forgive you, and I don't."

Her sad words validate Blaise Pascal's classic assumption: "There
is a God shaped vacuum in the heart of every man which cannot be
filled by any created thing, but only by God, the Creator, made known
through Jesus."

What Laski was looking for was "the bread of heaven," what Jesus
claimed to be. She was unable, or unwilling, to believe that there is a
God like Jesus and that Jesus could satisfy the emptiness of her life. She
was hungry for God.

She knew a lot about religion but did not know God. The Pharisees, according to Jesus, were in the same predicament. They were up
to their eyebrows in religion but they did not know God. They were
looking for a Messiah who would recognize their authority and their
righteousness, not one who would boldly declare that he had come
down from heaven to be living bread and living water.

The Pharisees wanted a Messiah who would do their will, not one
who would upset their apple carts by exposing their hypocrisy. After
all, the claims of Jesus were ludicrous; what right did he have to say

108

that he was the bread God had sent? Or that he was the living water? Such absurdity they could not accept!

Yet Jesus insisted that he was the true bread that satisfies and the water than quenches the thirst of all who follow him. Some in every age find this hard to believe just as the Jews balked at believing it.

Admittedly no one can accept Jesus' claims except by faith. But that is exactly what God asks for – faith! Genuine faith enables Christians to believe that Jesus is everything he says he is and that he has the power to do all that he says he can do.

Seven times Jesus says emphatically "I am." We have to decide how to respond to his claims. We can decide that he was confused or crazy. We can decide that this was the Gospel writer John talking, not Jesus. Or we can decide that what Jesus said is true. This is the choice of faith. It is a decision, the Bible says, that enables a person to receive forgiveness for their sins and be reconciled to God. To do so is to eat living bread that satisfies the hunger of the soul for peace with God.

Most of us know the contentment of being satisfied with physical bread. Our hunger is gone. We want no more. Partaking of Jesus as the living bread provides that same satisfaction spiritually. A popular hymn expresses that contentment with this lovely phrase: "Bread of heaven, feed me till I want no more!"

Once it was my privilege to host a Methodist bishop from India on a visit to America. His words still ring in my ears: "In my land many are starving; they are hungry for bread for their bodies. But they have a greater need – to know Jesus so their souls can be nourished by the Bread of heaven."

The enjoyment of a good meal is temporary; hunger will soon return. But the bread of heaven provides a more lasting satisfaction. Another word for this soul satisfaction is peace, the peace that believers experience when Jesus fills the vacuum in the heart. This peace is an inward assurance that our "eternal life" has already begun.

When my friend John Felton was dying, he did not tell me about his suffering, his politics or his accomplishments. He told me about Jesus. He said simply, "Pastor, Jesus is everything."

I think that is what Jesus meant by claiming to be living bread and living water. To have him is to have everything we need – now and forever. The claims of Jesus are indeed astounding but the hungers of the heart are never satisfied until you believe those claims.

If this is true then we ought not to keep it a secret! + + +

43

Love always wins

June is the popular month for weddings. I have presided over a thousand weddings. Sometimes the couple asked me to read verses from Paul's First Letter to the Corinthians, chapter 13.

It is one of the most beautiful chapters in the Bible. But I must confess that this scripture humbles me. Every time I read this chapter I wilt under its judgment of my life. But whenever I confess that inadequacy to the Inner Voice, he always whispers: "Relax, Walter; it's not about you, it's about me and the agape love I can pour into you when you trust and obey me." In that moment I enjoy again the sweet relief that comes only on the wings of amazing grace.

To understand the kind of love Paul describes in this chapter we need the help of several Greek words used for love in the first century. The New Testament was written in the language of the common people, Koine Greek. This language used four words to describe different kinds of love.

Eros was the word used for sexual love. We get our word "erotic" from this word. Storge was used to explain family affection. Philia is the word for the affection Christian friends have for one another. We might call it brotherly love.

The fourth word is agape, the noblest form of love, the kind of love God has for his children. Agape love wants the best for others; it's the kind of love Jesus demonstrated. He even loved his enemies and prayed for them as they were crucifying him. Agape love was what kept Jesus from giving up on his disciples even when they denied knowing him.

Anyone who has tried it knows how difficult it is to practice agape love in daily living. In chapter 13 Paul explains what agape love looks like. It is kind and patient. It does not envy or boast. It is not rude or self-seeking. It is not easily angered. It keeps no record of wrongs. That kind of challenge leaves most of us gasping for breath! But this is how God wants us to live, and he will not let us off the hook with the flimsy excuse that "I'm only human."

So how do we deal with this dilemma? The answer is clear: we have to embrace the truth that agape love is a gift of God. We can only receive it; we cannot manufacture it. We cannot make it happen by trying harder. We must admit that, without God's help, we cannot possibly love in the way God expects us to love.

None of the spiritual gifts is anything apart from love. All of life must be grounded in love or we will spend our days missing the mark. We should examine carefully what Paul says in chapter 13. If I can speak in the prayer language of an angel but not have love, then I am nothing but noise! Great knowledge and great faith do not impress God if love is missing. Paul leaves no room for doubt about what he means: If I "do not have love, I am nothing"!

When I read this chapter and insert my name, Walter, in the place of the word "love," it drives me to my knees. This is how God expects me to live but I fail so often. My response is usually, "Lord, forgive me. Such love is impossible for me."

But then I hear the Inner Voice saying, "Yes, it is impossible for you to love like this in your own strength. But when you are yielded to me, and willing to receive my love into your heart, then all things are possible!"

In such moments I remember the eternal nature of love. The things I have accumulated will perish. None of my earthly treasures will escape decay and destruction. But love will last forever! It "will never end" because God is love.

Love will abide when everything else is gone! Nothing is greater than love. The best news, in the midst of the perplexities of life, is that love always wins! And if I am willing God will help me receive and share his agape love with others. +

44

Called to be ministers

I was a grown man before I understood that all Christians are called to "the ministry," not just preachers. And it was a Quaker, not a Methodist, who helped me embrace the idea that every Christian is a minister. A Quaker philosopher, Elton Trueblood helped me see that the word "minister" means much more than "preacher." My eyes were opened to the biblical truth that every disciple of Jesus is called to engage in the ministry of Christ. The work of Christ is too great an assignment for ordained clergy alone. God's plan is for all believers to live as Christ's ministers no matter what their vocation.

We may enlarge the idea by changing the word "minister" to "servant." Every Christian is a servant of Christ. All believers are called to live as servants of Christ. Combine the terms and we may say that every Christian is a ministering servant of Christ. The New Testament teaches us that Christians are expected to serve others in love.

In washing the dirty feet of his disciples Jesus modeled the humble way he expects his followers to serve others. By washing the disciples' feet Jesus got their attention. Peter was stunned, unwilling at first for Jesus to wash his feet. After Jesus explained what the washing meant, Peter was more than eager for the Master to wash his feet.

Jesus used the occasion to explain that he was setting an example for the disciples. He knew they would not soon forget what he had done. Washing feet was dirty work usually done by slaves. The disciples could hardly believe their eyes when Jesus picked up the towel and basin and began "serving" them. In doing so he was their servant. And he was teaching them how he wanted them to live.

If you have ever participated in a "foot-washing" service, you know how uncomfortable it is to have someone wash your feet. It is a humbling and deeply emotional experience. The Spirit often moves people to tears as sins are confessed amid cries for forgiveness and reconciliation.

I remember a time when a woman in a retreat knelt in front of her husband, and washing his feet gently, asked forgiveness for her rotten attitude. After she returned to her seat, her husband knelt before her, and washed her feet with water and his own tears. He asked her to forgive him for all the ways he had hurt her for many years. Needless to say, we "had church" that night. To witness two people forgiving each other is truly to see God at work. That is what church is all about.

Trueblood has called Mark 10:45 "the most revolutionary verse in the Bible." It is revolutionary because most of us are "control freaks." We want to be in charge; we want others to serve us. We think we know how everything should be done and we need no advice from others about how to run the ship. Unlike Jesus, we have come to be served. Humble servanthood is not our game.

Yet we have no choice if we desire to be authentic followers of Christ. Those who follow him are servants of others. They wash feet, pure and simple. Washing feet is not an optional course for believers. It is part of the core curriculum for kingdom dwellers. Is that not the primary lesson we have learned from Albert Schweitzer and Mother Teresa? Both of them knew how to wash feet. They modeled humble servanthood.

There are many ways to "wash feet." Jim does it by doing the weekly grocery shopping for a home-bound neighbor. Ron does it by being available 24-7 to a friend who is recovering from drug addiction. Susan does it by cooking and delivering meals for people who are home recovering from serious surgery. John does it by cutting the lawn for an injured neighbor who is no longer able to mow his own grass. Those who do it best find simple ways to share the love of Christ with their neighbors.

You might look around for someone whose feet you could wash. If you see no one you might need to ask Jesus to wash your feet. His "cleansing" often opens our eyes to the opportunities we have to wash feet as his humble servants. We make our Lord known by washing feet. Surely he is pleased when we follow his example. +

45

You have got to be kidding!

Life is difficult. One trial after another seems to be the norm. And how do we react to trouble? You know the answer. We ask the question, "Why did God allow this to happen to me?" Or we blame someone else for our troubles.

Christians tell us we can find help for our trials in the Bible. So we turn to the New Testament. We learn that Jesus says, "In this world you will have trouble, but be of good cheer." It's the "good cheer" part that causes us difficulty. How do you manage to be cheerful when your world is falling apart?

James, the brother of Jesus, should be able to help us. He was close to Jesus. So we turn to James' New Testament letter and find him saying we should welcome our troubles with joy! To which I must say, "You have got to be kidding!"

James, however, is not kidding. He says joy and he means joy. And his advice carries a lot of weight. After all, his teaching comes from the Bible, the greatest book ever written. So let's wrestle with what he says and try to make sense of this business of being joyful in the midst of stress.

James puts a lot of stock in faith. But faith does not prevent trouble. James tells us that God tests our faith with trials. He allows trouble to test our faith. But during these tests God is with us; James is confident that in the midst of our trials, God is with us!

That makes sense. And that is a comforting thought. After all, God's name is Immanuel, the beautiful name that means "God with us." As long as we can believe God is with us we can handle most any trial that comes up.

James teaches that God uses our testing times to make us stronger. And he uses our trials to teach us patience. This is similar to Saint Paul's teaching that "tribulation produces patience."

Sometimes we jokingly say, "Lord, I believe I am patient enough; please do not send me any more tribulation!" Even so, we have to admit that we learn more, and grow more, from difficult times than we do when life is easy.

Recognizing this we gradually learn that what we really need is not an easy life but a life filled with God working in us – to make us what we ought to be. That brings to mind that wonderful Gaither song for children: "He's still working on me, to make me what I ought to be." That is a marvelous idea: that the God who made me, who loves me, is forever working on me! And often he uses people who are like sandpaper to rub off our rough edges!

Questions arise in times of testing. But instead of asking why God allowed our troubles to happen, we might more wisely ask, "What does God want me to learn from this test of my faith? Perhaps that is why James urges us to ask God for wisdom. God alone can help us understand why certain trials come. Human wisdom is not enough.

Godly wisdom helps us better understand the true meaning of patience. To be patient is not simply to take things in stride stoically. The patience James speaks about involves strength of character and the faith to persevere rather than surrender.

Thomas Samford, legal counsel for Auburn University for 30 years, demonstrated to his family and friends that one can welcome trials with joy. Diagnosed with terminal cancer, and advised he had about a year to live, Thomas refused to think of himself as a victim; he welcomed his affliction with joyous faith. Remarkably, he lived a dozen more years though in a continual struggle with cancer.

I was one of Thomas' pastors. He and I began to meet with a few other men at 6:30 on Wednesday mornings. This time of sharing and prayer became one of the great blessings of my life and the other men shared this conviction. I never had any difficulty getting up early on Wednesday mornings, knowing that a man who was struggling with cancer and chemotherapy would be waiting for me to pick him up. His remarkable courage inspired all who knew Thomas.

We will never forget Thomas saying, "I thank God for my cancer. My cancer led me to know God. Except for my cancer, I would have missed meeting the Master. I am not fighting cancer," he would tell us. "I am simply asking for grace and strength to teach His Word until He is ready for me to come home. Whatever time and energy He gives me, I will use to please Him." And he did!

When Thomas died I realized that as much as anyone I have ever known he had lived out the wisdom of James: *"Consider it pure joy, my brothers, whenever you face trials of many kinds, because you know that the testing of your faith develops perseverance."*

At Thomas' funeral I quoted these words from James: *"Blessed is the man who perseveres under trial, because when he has stood the test, he will receive the crown of life that God has promised to those who love him."*

Thomas had "stood the test" and I believe he received from God the promised "crown of life." Ever since Thomas departed this life I have been asking God to help me welcome my trials with joy so that one day it can be said of me, "He stood the test – and he stood it with joy." +

46

Should the church entertain us?

Some people do not go to church because they find the worship services boring. I understand that complaint. I have gone to sleep in church several times. The monotonous sound of a preacher's voice can put people to sleep. And I must admit that I have preached sermons that had I been in the audience I would probably have gone to sleep.

Those of us who are pastors should be ashamed that sometimes we have offered worship services that were about as exciting as watching paint dry. We know in our hearts there is no excuse for worship that is devoid of passion and enthusiasm.

But before we lay all the blame at the feet of the pastors perhaps we should look at worship from another perspective. Some of us may have the wrong reason for going to church. We may, for example, be going to church to be entertained. That is one of the poorest of all reasons for going to church. Yet in a culture that craves entertainment many have mistakenly decided that the church should entertain us. And sadly some pastors have capitulated to this demand for entertainment.

Nowhere in the Bible does God counsel pastors to entertain those who come to worship. We are admonished "not to forsake the assembling of ourselves together." For what purpose, then, should we come together to worship? Even a cursory study of scripture reveals that the primary object of corporate worship should be to praise God. So our basic motivation for going to church should be to blend our voices with others in praise to God, out of gratitude for our salvation and for his strengthening presence in daily living.

The pastor's role is to design worship so that people are confronted, and comforted, by the Holy Scriptures. When this is done well, with passion and enthusiasm, worship is not boring.

Consider that one Sunday I am overwhelmed by guilt. A sense of my sinfulness has made me miserable. Then I hear the pastor read the story in Luke chapter seven of a sinful woman to whom Jesus says, "Your sins are forgiven." The pastor goes on to say that this same Jesus was raised from the dead by the power of God and he is here this morning ready to whisper in your heart: "Your sins are forgiven?" In that moment I repent of my sins. I believe that Jesus has forgiven me of my sins. Instantly the chains of sin that had bound me are broken; Jesus has set me free! My chains are gone! That, beloved, is not boring worship!

Such an experience on a Sunday morning motivates me to worship God every day – to praise him for the peace that comes from a restored relationship with my heavenly Father. We do not receive any brownie points for "going to church" one hour a week; what God desires for us is intimate, daily fellowship with him through his Son who died for our sins.

True worship is not sitting in church as though you are the "inspector general," there to evaluate what others are doing. True worship is bringing your life before God moment by moment and saying with sincerity, "Here am I, Lord, I am your servant; thank you for the joy of my salvation, for the peace that passes understanding. Show me today how to do your will so that I may honor and please you."

Real worship is sharing God's tender compassion for the poor, the lost, the lame, the blind, the suffering and saying to the Father, "Where can I join hands with you in helping hurting people?" Get into a life like that and what happens on Sunday morning at eleven o'clock will become more exciting than you ever dreamed! +

47

When you feel trapped

Optimism is good. Positive thinking is the best kind. I enjoy being around positive people who smile and affirm that "Life is good." I need friends who remind me daily that life is too short to allow much of it to be spoiled by pessimism.

When asked how he is feeling one of my friends always replies, "If I felt any better I would be twins!" He delights in being positive. People like people with a positive attitude.

Even when life is tough we can be thankful for our blessings. Helen Keller once said: "So long as the memory of certain beloved friends lives in my heart, I shall say that life is good." Bravo, Helen, you were right! Most of us have reasons enough to declare, life is good!

However realism demands we admit that sometimes life is bad. It can be really bad. Terrible things happen to people, things that are difficult to explain and things that cause us to feel trapped.

Most of us feel trapped at times. Illness can trap us, especially if the doctor is puzzled about how to treat us. Our sins can trap us. We tell a lie and it leads to another. Then the truth emerges and we feel trapped.

We live beyond our means and our debts trap us. A colleague at work becomes impossible to work with and reconciliation seems hopeless. Injury results in physical confinement and doctors offer no hope of recovery.

To feel free as the wind is a marvelous feeling. To feel trapped, sometimes by circumstances not of our own making, is a dreadful feeling that can bring us to our knees. But that may be the very place we need to be – on our knees, finally ready to let the good Lord help us escape. One man said, "I had to get to the end of my resources before I discovered God's resources."

Catherine Marshall once wrote a book titled *Adventures in Prayer*. In it she offers some helpful prayers, like this one:

"Lord, I have been defeated by circumstances. I have felt like an animal trapped in a corner with nowhere to flee. Where are YOU in all this, Lord? The night is dark. I cannot feel your presence.

"Help me to know that the darkness is really 'shade of your hand, outstretched caressingly;' that the 'hemming in' is your doing. Perhaps there was no other way you could get my full attention, no other way I would allow you to demonstrate what you can do in my life.

"I see now that the emptier my cup is, the more space there is to receive your love and supply. Lord, I hand to you my situation, asking you to fill it from your bountiful reservoirs in your own time and your own way.

"How I thank you, Father in heaven, that your riches are available to me, not on the basis of my deserving, but of Jesus and his worthiness. Therefore, in the strength of his name I pray. Amen."

That is the kind of prayer I need to pray from time to time. I need to remember when I feel trapped that the good Lord is in the business of setting prisoners free. And he has the power to set me free. Then, in spite of pain and misfortune, I can sing and shout in the darkness that because God loves us, life really is good, mighty good! +

48

Do all the good you can

I have been a Methodist all my life. And all my life I have treasured this quotation from John Wesley, the founder of Methodism:

"Do all the good you can, by all the means you can, in all the ways you can, in all the places you can, at all the times you can, to all the people you can, as long as ever you can."

Imagine my surprise to learn recently that John Wesley did not say that. One of our respected Wesleyan scholars insists that you cannot find that statement anywhere in Wesley's writings.

I will take the good scholar's word for that. But though the statement may have been erroneously attributed to Wesley, it is still an excellent piece of advice – especially for those who follow Jesus.

When we truly belong to Jesus, we do our best to follow the example of our Lord. And the Bible says Jesus "went about doing good."

Instead of looking out for their own interests, Christ followers will constantly look for people they can help – physically, emotionally or spiritually. Sometimes the help people need is a listening ear and a caring heart. Sometimes it is a word of encouragement. At other times it may be a month's rent when a person on a fixed income has been overwhelmed by medical expenses.

Saint Paul understood that you can become weary serving others. Even the noblest Christians can become exhausted in "doing good." However, Paul has no sympathy for us. His remedy when we are tempted by weariness: resist it! Refuse to be discouraged! "Do not grow weary in doing what is right"! He reminds us that there is a reward for faithfulness: if we do not give up, we shall reap a harvest because God is faithful!

Ultimately there are only two ways to live. One is the way of the flesh that leads to death. The other is the way of the Spirit that leads to life. One is the way of selfishness, the other the way of love. In the end, love wins. Schuyler Colfax, Vice-Present under President Grant, understood this:

"Man derives his greatest happiness not by that which he does for himself, but by what he accomplishes for others. This is a sad world at best – a world of sorrow, of suffering, of injustice, and falsification. Men stab those whom they hate with the stiletto of slander. But it is for the followers of our Lord to improve it, and to make it more as Christ would have it. The most precious crown of fame that a human being can ask is to kneel at the bar of God and hear the beautiful words, 'Well done, good and faithful servant.'" He was right.

The words on an old plaque in an antique store say it all: "Only one life, twill soon be past; only what's done for Christ will last."

I reckon trying to live like Jesus lived is about the best way to live. Though it is impossible to do it perfectly, we can try. And when we make the effort unseen hands will help us. +

49

The beautiful influence of a friend

Across the years few people inspired me more than Elton Trueblood, the noted Quaker author, theologian, preacher and philosophy of religion professor. He was 70 and already retired from teaching when at age 38 I met him.

His wit and winsome personality impressed me but I was awed most by his disciplined way of living. He was orderly in every way imaginable. He shared the conviction of John Wesley that one should never waste time in idleness.

When he learned that I aspired to become a writer, he asked when I did my writing. I was floored by his simple question and embarrassed by my answer.

I said meekly, "Whenever I can find the time." He chose not to chide me though his momentary silence was a gentle rebuff. Quietly he said, "I write every Thursday. I find it necessary to set aside a time every week to devote myself to serious writing."

He did not go on to tell me I needed such a plan. There was no need to do that. He realized that his point had been made and that no reasonable argument could refute it. Skill in writing results from the disciplined use of one's time.

In the years since that conversation I have struggled not to "find" time for writing but to dedicate weekly blocks of time for writing. Though time management is not easy, without it most of our goals can never be realized.

Trueblood taught me the value of punctuality. He never kept people waiting. When I spent two weeks with him at Earlham College he invited me to meet with him every morning at eight am. If he said eight o'clock, he meant eight o'clock, not five minutes after eight.

For ten days I met him at his study at eight every morning. We shared together for an hour. At nine o'clock he excused himself to attend to other duties. I was never late and he was always there when I arrived.

When Trueblood stood to deliver a sermon he always pulled out his pocket watch and placed it on the pulpit. Twenty minutes later he was done. He had a plan and he stuck to it. He was organized but even more he was brilliantly effective. His messages were relevant, riveting and persuasive. I found his preaching clear and compelling. I felt somehow God was speaking to my own heart every time I heard him preach.

I loved Trueblood's idea of living life "in chapters." He used that idea to write his autobiography, While It Is Day. It helps to "close" one chapter in your life and turn the page to begin a new chapter.

During his prime Trueblood was the most widely respected Quaker in America. His 35 books were written for the laity but his writing deeply influenced the clergy in most major denominations. He despised the word "laity" and the pulpit as well. Pulpits serve only to separate people, he said. He argued against the separation of persons as clergy and laity, insisting that "every Christian is a minister." This single idea became widespread and has profoundly affected Christianity in recent years.

Two of Elton's best books were *The Company of the Committed* and *The Incendiary Fellowship*. Both are still good reads for those who are serious about living a disciplined Christian life. I loved his book, *The Humor of Christ*. He also wrote a good book about Abraham Lincoln in which he described him as "a theologian of American anguish."

I am a better man because I met Elton Trueblood. His willingness to embrace me as a friend, and become my mentor, was one of the truly great blessings of my life. When he died at age 94, in 1994, I knelt in a quiet place and thanked God for his remarkable influence upon my life.

Some people touch our lives in beautiful ways. They inspire us to become better people. Somehow their influence makes the trials of life more bearable. + + +

50

Our special day

April 18 is a special day for me and my wife. It is not a holiday. It is not the birthday of a president or a Civil War general. For most people it is just another day on the calendar. But for us it is a special day every year because our first son was born that day in 1953.

Many Lee County Alabama residents will remember April 18, 1953 for a different reason. A vicious tornado ripped through east Alabama that day, destroying several homes and damaging many others.

Dean and I began married life in an upstairs apartment on College Street across from Auburn United Methodist Church. Dean was soon pregnant. After she fell down the stairs leading to our apartment we rented a house at 818 Lakeview Drive in Auburn. The rent was a whopping $75 per month. I was in my third year at API, the land-grant college that would later become known as Auburn University.

Early in the morning of April 18 we hurried off to the small hospital that is now called East Alabama Medical Center. Dean's sharp and increasingly rapid labor pains convinced her that today she would deliver her firstborn.

Dark clouds and the forecast of bad weather made us a little uneasy. But it was the turbulence of childbirth, not the weather, that got our attention that day.

The raging storm forced the hospital to switch to emergency power when nearby power lines went down. Rain was hitting the windows in torrents. Water even poured into the hospital through the air-conditioning ducts. Several hours would pass before we heard that a tornado had ripped through the community.

Our kind physician, Dr. Ben Thomas, had to drive through a torrential rain from Auburn to get to the hospital. Shortly after his arrival, debris from the storm made driving in the area quite hazardous.

When I returned home that night, elated by the safe delivery of our first son, I found our house had been damaged by the storm. The roof had been ripped off above the front door, allowing the rain to soak some of our furniture. But the damage seemed incidental compared to the total destruction of several nearby homes.

Weighing nine pounds and two ounces, our baby boy was beautiful and healthy. His blond hair and blue eyes made him even more special to us. We were thrilled to have started our family. Though we had little money, we enjoyed life. The future was bright. We had the world by the tail. I finished Auburn and we moved to Nashville where I enrolled in seminary at Vanderbilt University.

But soon another storm descended upon us just as swiftly as the tornado had come. Tests brought bad news. Our doctor's voice was breaking as he fought back tears and gave us the dreadful news, "Your son has leukemia."

He explained that there was no known cure. The best he could do would be to keep David comfortable until he died. "Perhaps," he said, "a cure will be discovered soon; a lot of research is being done."

I asked how long David might live. His answer sent a chill up and down my spine. "My best guess is somewhere between two months and two years," he said. It was the worst moment of my life – hearing that death sentence for our precious little boy. David was two years old, five months into his third year.

That diagnosis shattered our world on a day in September. David suffered. We struggled with the burden. We prayed. We cried. We stifled our anger and wrestled with our fear. Underneath all our frustration was the maddening question: Why would a loving God let a beautiful little boy die like this?

Finally David's suffering came to an end on a day in May the next year. His death wounded us but it did not destroy us. Though tested sorely by the loss of our only child, our marriage lasted and became stronger. God met us in the hallways of hell and showed us the way out. We refused to become bitter and asked God to make us better. We tried to let him use our pain.

Over the years since David's death our sadness has given way to the overwhelming joy that is God's gift to those who keep on holding his hand through tough times. And each time April 18 rolls around we pause to give thanks for the privilege of having David for three short years. We also give thanks that in his kindness, God gave us four other sons, each of whom is very precious to us.

Each April 18 as we celebrate David's birth we offer thanks that we are still together, still able to remember his beautiful smile and still thankful for the joy that was ours on the stormy day our first child was born. +

51

Finishing well

I have learned some valuable lessons from old people. From my youth I was taught to respect my elders. That was good advice because old people have a lot of wisdom to share with those who will listen.

There are many wise people in the Bible from whom we can learn. Solomon, for example, was so wise that his name is synonymous with wisdom. His life is worthy of serious reflection. We can learn wonderful lessons by "listening" to Solomon's teachings and we can learn from his example.

Solomon was just a boy when he was made king of Israel. Historians are not sure of his age when his father, King David, died. He may have been as young as 12, but not more than 20. David was a tough act to follow. He had established quite a reputation as a great king.

Solomon quickly won favor with the people. His attitude was rather stunning for a king. He admitted that he was but "a little boy" who hardly knew his way in and out of the house. So he asked God for understanding, the wisdom to rule well and to discern the difference between good and evil.

His request was made in response to a question he felt God was asking him, "What do you want me to give you?" What Solomon did not ask for is impressive. He did not ask for a long life or wealth. Nor did he ask for the death of his enemies. He asked for one thing: an understanding heart.

The Bible says that God was pleased and gave him what he asked for. In addition God gave him wealth and honor, promising him that "in your lifetime you will have no equal among kings." So, richly blessed by God, Solomon ruled for some 80 years. He built the great temple that his father had wanted to build as well as a splendid palace for himself.

Everyone atIf you want to examine Solomon's wisdom, read the
Book of Proverbs in the Bible. Jesus was so impressed with Solomon's
good judgment that he quoted him more than once. Here is one saying
that Jesus found worthy of reiterating:

*"Do not exalt yourself in the king's presence, and do not claim a
place among great men; it is better for him to say to you, 'Come up here,'
than for him to humiliate you before a nobleman"* (Proverbs 25:6-7,
NIV).

*The following sayings are delightful examples of Solomon's wise in-
sights:*

"An honest answer is like a kiss on the lips."

"A word aptly spoken is like apples of gold in settings of silver."

*"A fool gives full vent to his anger, but a wise man keeps himself
under control."*

*"Do you see a man who speaks in haste? There is more hope for a
fool than for him."*

*"Better to live on a corner of the roof than share a house with a
quarrelsome wife."*

This is one of my choice favorites:

*"A cheerful heart is good medicine, but a crushed spirit dries up the
bones."*

Solomon had great wisdom, wealth, power and influence. Yet his
life ended in disgrace. What happened? Simply this – he became overly
impressed with himself. Perhaps his kingly power intoxicated him to
the extent that he believed he did not have to follow the rules he believed other men should live by.

Instead of following God's advice about women, Solomon made
his own rules and did what he pleased. His is the story of a man who
had it all, but lost it before crossing the finish line. He was wise but in
his late years he became very foolish.

If, as someone has said, all you have left at the end of the day is
your name and your reputation, then Solomon is to be pitied. He had
a listening heart, an understanding mind, for most of his life, but he
stumbled and fell near the end of the race.

Will it matter that we had fame and fortune if along the way we lose the wisdom to finish well? My longtime friend Roy Jordan told me that before he retired, he resolved to do everything possible "to finish well." As I am nearing home that is my goal also – to do all within my power to finish well. Every wise man will do his best to finish well. +

52

A voice like thunder

We buried our boy in May. That summer we sought relief from our grief by taking a vacation at Lake Junaluska, North Carolina. Still a seminary student studying for the ministry, I persuaded my wife to go the week when Billy Graham was preaching.

Sitting under the ministry of Billy Graham for a few days would renew our faith. We admired his strong preaching. The death of our son had not broken us but our hearts were heavy. We needed a time of healing.

Billy Graham was as stirring as ever. The huge auditorium was packed morning and night as hundreds of people flocked to hear him. We stood in a long line one day and finally got to shake his hand. Like others we were awed by Graham's persuasive preaching.

Graham shared the pulpit with another preacher, W. E. Sangster from England. And it was Sangster whom God used that week to bring healing to my wounded heart. I was captivated by the power with which his words penetrated my heart. He spoke with unusual authority, intensity and conviction.

Every word he spoke had the ring of truth about it. It was as if God was speaking directly to my questioning mind and answering questions I had not even asked. Never had I been more convinced that God himself was speaking to me. I listened intently, eager to drink in what I was certain was eternal truth.

I had many questions. Why had God, if he is love, allowed our son to die? Why had he not healed him in answer to our prayers? Why should a little child have to suffer when he had done no wrong? Why had God given him to us if he was going to take him from us before he could grow up? Was his death punishment for my own sins? Is God really "out there" and if he is, why doesn't he say something when I beg him for help?

Finally God did reply. He was silent when David was suffering. Now, two months after our son's burial, God spoke. He spoke through Sangster. How do I know? I know. I was there. Though it happened nearly 60 years ago, I remember it like it was yesterday. God answered me through the voice of his servant, an English preacher named Sangster.

I had felt sorry for Sangster. He would be no match for Billy Graham as a presence in the pulpit. But I was wrong. Sangster was older and wiser than Graham. And though his style was quite different, the man could preach. As the week went on, many of us realized we were listening to two of the world's greatest preachers.

What did I hear from God? Not what I wanted to hear, believe me. I wanted something soothing; what I got was disturbing.

Sangster said, "You must stop dealing with your problems. You must deal with God! You get nowhere by grappling with cancer or some tragedy. You must wrestle with God for God is the sovereign God of the universe and he allows whatever happens to you. He does not will evil but he allows it. The world is not out of control; God is in control and he allows bad things to happen." For me that was an entirely new concept.

He went on to insist that God has a purpose in allowing tragedy even though we may never understand why he allows it. We can find peace only by accepting God's sovereignty in our lives and believing that in all things he is always working for our good. God is not accountable to us for his actions; on the contrary, we are accountable to God for our actions and reactions. And God loves us even when he allows bad things to happen in our lives.

As much as I was able I surrendered my stubborn, agnostic questioning to God that week. I began to rethink our son's death in a new way, a way that helped me see suffering in a new light. Slowly I tried to embrace the message God gave me through a preacher I would never hear again. His message was the strong medicine my sick heart needed.

A few years later word came from England that Sangster was dying, having lost his voice to a muscular disease that was paralyzing his nervous system. The great pulpit voice would soon be silent in the grave. But before his death, he wrote a simple message to his new friend Billy Graham: "Tell people that the gospel works when a man is dying."

I have journeyed to Lake Junaluska many times, heard many inspiring speakers, and enjoyed the beauty of those North Carolina hills. But never have I been as deeply moved as I was that summer in 1956. On a clear day I can close my eyes and still hear the thundering voice of W. E. Sangster reverberating within the walls of Stuart Auditorium. It was a time when God spoke – and I heard him. +

53

Kids love to hear grandma's yarns

Mama and I have nine great grandchildren. We love for them to come to see us and sometimes we are glad to see them leave. The older ones are fascinated with stories that mama can tell about her childhood. Grandma Dean can reel off story after story about her mother's mother and the hard times folks endured back in the good old days.

I enjoy her stories too, especially the ones about her Grandmother Emma. Emma raised nine children in the backwoods of Tallapoosa County, Alabama. All of them lived into their nineties until all that lard Emma fed them finally put them in the ground. Too much fat will kill you eventually.

Cool water in a creek near the house served as their refrigerator. After all, the only running water they had was the water that ran by in that creek. Indoor plumbing was only a dream. Like most families they had a well-worn path to the outhouse. Pouring in a sack of lime occasionally helped a little with the nauseating stench.

When the cows were milked, the milk was poured into earthenware jugs and carefully placed in a shaded, shallow place in the creek where it stayed until mealtime. Other items, like bottles of "soda water" and other perishables were also cooled in the creek. The water was clean and safe enough to drink. At least they believed it was safe.

Butter and buttermilk were obtained not with money but with muscles – churning the milk in those old churns that are now on sale in every flea market. Churning was one of the chores assigned to Emma's girls. The older boys were spared from churning; it was their job to care for and feed the livestock. Younger lads would sometimes take their turn at the churn but they always grumbled that it was "women's work."

Grampa finally grubbed enough off the land to buy Emma an icebox. No longer were they forced to walk back and forth to the creek. The only trouble was, the ice soon melted. Now, instead of trips to the creek, they had to make frequent visits to the Ice House in town to purchase blocks of ice. Naturally Grampa complained about how expensive it was to own that icebox.

Years later, not long before she died, Emma swapped her icebox for a fancy refrigerator. Her wood-burning stove was another matter. She continued cooking on it until they put her in a nursing home. She simply did not trust those electric stoves.

Emma had her doubts too about the refrigerator. She and Grampa had used a smokehouse for years. They were sure it tasted better than that "store-bought" meat. When the men killed a hog, they took the meat to the smokehouse while it was still warm. There it was salted and stored away for the curing. My wife remembers hearing Emma's children say that they used black pepper, red pepper, and molasses, along with plenty of salt, to cure the meat. Of course the smoke also helped.

Emma never bought three pair of socks for five dollars at Wal-Mart. Instead she knitted socks for the whole family with her own knitting needle. When a hole was worn in the socks, Emma patched the hole with her busy needle.

Flour was sold in large sacks in the old days. The sacks sometimes had a colorful design on them, pretty enough for the sacks to be made into cute dresses for the girls. That custom lingered on for many years; my wife remembers that she and her sister also wore flour-sack dresses when they were growing up.

Grandma Dean feels a strange kinship with Grandma Emma. She can imagine her sitting by a winter fire, cooking and sewing for her large family, and telling stories since there was no television to watch. Dean enjoys her fireplace in our home. She has refused to let me change to gas logs. She likes to sit like Emma once sat, pondering life before burning logs. A fire mesmerizes her soul, inspiring her to imagine life as it was so long ago for her kin.

Most of us would like to make the world a better place. We can, but only if we recognize that our legacy reaches back many centuries, all the way to the folks who made the first wheel.

Countless generations have come and gone, each leaving a precious deposit of memories and achievements. The progress of civilization depends upon each of us doing what we can to make life better for our heirs. We are stewards of the past with the opportunity to add to our rich heritage.

One day I hope to meet Grandma Emma and sit on a cloud for a hundred years listening to her stories about churns, ice boxes and hard times. I am indebted to Emma because my wife inherited some of her genes. Dean's strengths suggest that she and Emma would have been good friends, and goodness knows the stories they might have shared around a roaring fire on a winter evening. +

54

A greenhorn preacher

Mega churches are popular these days. People are impressed with big screens, exciting contemporary music and world-famous preachers proclaiming the gospel. But lest we forget let me put in a good word for the contribution of our small country churches.

They are the training ground for new preachers. I know that from personal experience. A greenhorn if there ever was one, at age 21 I became the pastor of four small churches near Milstead, Alabama. Honestly I did not have a clue about what to do.

I had no training for the job. The Methodist hierarchy, after asking me to read and report on four books, issued me a license to preach. While still a student at Auburn University I got a call from Dr. W. F. Calhoun, then superintendent of the Montgomery District. He wanted to appoint me pastor of the LaPlace Circuit at a salary of $1900 a year. They would provide a parsonage in which we could live and continue my studies at Auburn. On very short notice I accepted the job.

The position was open in midyear because the pastor of the four churches had abruptly quit the ministry. Six weeks was enough for him. He left in the middle of a hot August night without even saying goodbye. No one ever understood why. And nobody seemed sorry that he had hit the road.

The good people of those churches were not surprised that I was a babe in the woods. All their pastors had been student pastors for many years. They were patient and expected me to learn on the job.

Learn I did. One of my churches was the old LaPlace Church, one of the earliest Methodist churches organized in Alabama. The church was just off Highway 80 in Shorter, now the home of the famous VictoryLand Greyhound Park and gambling casino. On a good Sunday 30 to 40 people showed up for worship at the LaPlace Church.

One of the faithful worshipers was Wright Noble. He appeared to be a pillar of the church so I decided one Sunday morning to call on him to pray. At the time, I was not comfortable praying or preaching. I figured I could use some help.

I learned that day never to call on someone to pray in church without asking permission beforehand. From the pulpit, I asked politely, "Mr. Noble, will you lead us in prayer?"

Without a moment's hesitation, he stood up and replied in a strong, firm voice, "I beg to be excused; that's what we pay the preacher for!"

Embarrassed and caught off guard, I stumbled through a prayer while most of my parishioners were quietly chuckling. I had no doubt that Mr. Noble was a Christian. I am sure he was a praying man. However, I never heard him pray.

My training for pastoral work had begun. Mr. Noble and others like him made sure that I understood why they paid my salary. There were certain things I was expected to do, none of which was ever explained to me in a "job description." They were quite willing for me to learn my duties, one at a time, in one embarrassing moment after another.

People pay the preacher for many reasons. Some pay him to mind his own business and that does not include "running the church." I had it explained to me more than once like this: "You stick to preaching the gospel and we will run the church."

In one of the churches I asked the church treasurer for a report on the offerings. He said, "We are fine, preacher, just fine." I asked, "Do you make a monthly report to the Board?" He replied, "No, I just let everybody know if we get behind. Right now, everything is fine." I think he kept the church's money in a cigar box, but I never found out. He taught me that it was none of my business how much money the church had in the bank.

I remembered that incident in the distant past when a pastor told me a similar story. He is being reassigned partly because of a bitter struggle with his church treasurer. In this case, the treasurer has refused to let anyone see the books. The preacher's demand to see the books cost him his job.

Most preachers feel like I do about being paid. I was always amazed that I could be paid to have so much fun. Our work is not drudgery and we are not in the ministry for the money. Many of us feel that we are paid far more than we deserve. And some of our parishioners are sure of it!

A retired preacher friend of mine was asked by a senior pastor to come on his staff as the minister of visitation, mainly to care for the sick and shut-in persons.

He replied, "You don't have enough money to hire me to visit the hospitals. When I was a pastor, the church paid me my full salary to visit the sick; I preached for free!"

A preacher gets paid to do many things. People have a thousand expectations of their preacher. Some people feel like they are not getting their money's worth; others wish they could pay the pastor more.

It is good when the preacher and the people can work together as a team, shepherding people with love. Key leaders who don't trust their pastor should find one they can trust by joining another church. Teamwork is essential.

The pastor, after all, is not a hired hand and he must never allow himself to become the private chaplain of the prominent "power brokers" – no matter how much he is paid. +

55

Mother Teresa may have been right

Some folks may disagree but I think I have a rather positive disposition. I try hard not to behave like a grumpy old man. I like people. I want people to like me. And I am quite certain that people do not enjoy negative people. So I make an effort to smile and be pleasant in my interaction with other people.

However in our increasingly impersonal society "being pleasant" is not a high priority for some people. Therein is my problem. It frustrates me when my kind words are rebuffed with a gruff reply. But what bothers me even more is that I often allow an apathetic reply to trigger a similar response from me.

My wife tries to help me. She says, "You should accept the world like it is. People don't owe you a smile. Stop expecting people to react the way you think they should. Just accept people the way they are and move on." She is right. I know it. But I just can't get over wanting people to be nice and friendly.

I realize I cannot control how other people act. I only have control of my actions and reactions. That is true. Still I have this nagging desire for people to be agreeable and kind.

I even believe I have a right to expect salespeople in the stores to be pleasant. Am I expecting too much? I don't think so. Here's the way I see it. Stores cannot exist without customers. I am a customer. I walk into a store with money. The salesclerk will not have a job unless customers like me spend money. Surely the people who need my money will offer me a warm and friendly greeting.

Guess what? The pleasant welcome is frequently not offered. The other day I walked into one of the popular big chain drugstores. Going to the pharmacy counter I handed a woman my prescription. No smile. No pleasant words. Just the blunt statement: "You don't bring that here; take it the drop-off counter." She pointed in that direction with a look that seemed to say, "Over there stupid!"

The woman at the drop-off counter was no improvement. No hello. No how are you. Without saying a word or looking me in the eyes she simply held out her hand. After giving her the paper I asked her long I might have to wait. She said dryly, "Probably 20 minutes."

After 20 minutes I was back at the first counter. Still no friendly smile from the "no nonsense" clerk. No sign that she was pleased that I was spending $110 for the medicine. If anything she seemed irritated that she had to explain their routine of having customers sign for the receipt of the medicine. Holding the bag of medicine in her hand she asked me to prove my identity before handing the bag to me. She was making sure I was not a gangster stealing someone's medicine.

When the transaction was completed she said without any feeling, and without looking at me, "Have a nice day." I managed a quiet "You too" as I walked away, nursing my wounded feelings. I was thinking, "Lord, help me stay well so I won't have to come back here anytime soon."

There is something wrong with that scene in the drugstore. A customer spending money to help make a business successful ought to be able to walk away feeling appreciated. Am I wrong to think somebody should have let me know they were glad I chose to spend my money in their store?

When I encounter the impersonal and sometimes unfriendly attitudes I try to give people the benefit of the doubt. Maybe the unpleasant clerk's husband had beaten her the night before, or perhaps she was suffering from hemorrhoids. Maybe there was a sick child at home. Pain and trouble do rob us of our joy so I need to remember that when I fault someone for not being pleasant.

My greatest concern is actually not with the attitudes of others but with my own. It bothers me that I am so quick to lose my own smile and my own pleasant disposition when I run into someone who is unfriendly and uncaring. That is the challenge for me – to maintain a cheerful attitude and not allow an unpleasant person to rob me of my congenial spirit.

Mother Teresa may have been right. She said the whole thing is between me and God, not between me and the unpleasant people. Here are her penetrating words:

People are often unreasonable and self-centered.
   Forgive them anyway.
If you are kind, people may accuse you of ulterior motives.
   Be kind anyway.
If you are honest, people may cheat you.
   Be honest anyway.
If you find happiness, people may be jealous.
   Be happy anyway.
The good you do today may be forgotten tomorrow.
   Do good anyway.
Give the world the best you have and it may never be enough.
   Give your best anyway.
For you see, in the end, it is between you and God.
It was never between you and them anyway.

I hate to admit it but the dear Mother's words nail me every time I read them. She was right. And I know the more I follow her advice the less unpleasant faces will frustrate me. Lord, help me! +

56

Small acts of kindness

Kindness makes a difference. Most people are cheered by kindness, especially when it not expected. Everyone is capable of performing acts of kindness and most of the time the gift of kindness costs us little or nothing.

Add to that the fact that kindness actually benefits the giver as well as the recipient. Scientific research has proven that being kind to others will improve your health. Acts of kindness release endorphins in the brain that boost the level of happiness for both the giver and the receiver. That may be one reason why Aesop said, "No act of kindness, no matter how small, is ever wasted."

Harold Kushner explains it even more clearly: "When you carry out acts of kindness you get a wonderful feeling inside. It is as though something inside your body responds and says yes, this is how I ought to feel."

I am not the first, of course, to make a case for kindness. Mark Twain did so when he said, "Kindness is a language which the deaf can hear and the blind can see." Like so many things Twain said, I wish I had said that.

Bob Hope, a genius at twisting a phrase, once said, "If you haven't any charity in your heart, you have the worst kind of heart trouble." You can smile and say amen to the words of a comedian who spent his life trying to make people smile.

Small acts of kindness can be simple things like holding a door open for someone walking behind you or even smiling at a store clerk who is serving you. Often a smile can chase away a frown. But even when it does not, you will feel better for having smiled.

Birthday cards can be acts of kindness especially if they contain a handwritten note of appreciation for someone's lasting friendship.

On a recent anniversary we received many cards from friends that must have released a truckload of those endorphins in our brains. We've been married so long that our friends can't believe we are still alive – and they remind us of that with crazy cards – which make us smile! Of course some of our friends are, like us, as old as dirt and they know it.

At annual conference in June a woman asked if she could sit with us. We were delighted by this small act of kindness by our friend Pat Caylor. As she sat with us, listening to the bishop announce the appointments of his preachers, we felt a surge of joy in our hearts. On a June day in 1952 Pat's mother, Bertha Bell, sang at our wedding. The kindness of her daughter in choosing to sit beside us was a precious anniversary gift.

King David was a great sinner who having confessed his sins experienced forgiveness because of the kindness of God. David gave us a beautiful word in the King James Version of the Bible when he wrote often of God's "lovingkindness."

Modern translations have changed that word to simply "love." I realize that "lovingkindness" is a cumbersome union of two words. But honestly I can think of few more beautiful verses in the Bible than Psalm 63:3 – "Because thy lovingkindness is better than life, my lips will praise thee." Surely it is the loving kindness of God that triggers in us the desire to offer others gifts of kindness.

Any day, like this very day, is a good day to perform small acts of kindness that will bless those around us, whether strangers or friends. I will allow Ralph Waldo Emerson to have the last word: "You cannot do a kindness too soon, for you never know how soon it will be too late." +

57

I have seen my Dad a lot lately

Strange as it may seem I have seen my Dad a lot lately. I saw him last night at a barbeque grill in the backyard of the home he built in 1930. He was grilling hamburgers.

Actually the person at the grill was my grandson Jake, now a senior at Auburn University. While Jake was expertly cooking burgers and dogs I saw my Dad doing the same thing, near that same spot, when I was a boy. There was one difference. Dad's grill was at ground level; the coals were in a hole he had dug in the earth. Jake's grill was built up with bricks two feet off the ground.

Inside the house Dean and I sat and talked with Jake's parents, our son Steve and his wife Amy. They live in the old home place, having bought and remodeled it after my parents died. We were celebrating their son Josh's graduation from Macon-East Academy and the opportunity given him to move on and play baseball for AUM (Auburn University in Montgomery).

The room in which we sat is their bedroom now, with a nice new bathroom built off the south side. It had been the bedroom of my parents during 50 of their 67 years of marriage.

Sitting there I saw my Dad struggling in his late years to get out of bed. He wanted so much to maintain his independence. But his strength was failing as he moved into his nineties. I remembered the day he said, "I could get out of bed by myself if only I had something to grab hold of."

My son Tim and I bought some pipe and fastened it to the floor just a foot away from Dad's bed. He was pleased. For a while he was able to grab that pipe and get out of bed and on his feet without assistance. The pipe looked strange but Dad liked it because it enabled him to help himself. I saw him using that pipe the other night in that bedroom.

In that very room I also saw my mother during the two years she remained after Dad died. Most of that time she was in a hospital bed in that room. Dad's prayers were for the most part answered. He had asked the Lord to let him live so he could take care of Mama. The Lord let him live into his 93rd year.

When we sit at Steve's and Amy's table to eat I see my Dad sitting in his familiar place in the room we called the "breakfast room." Whether it is planned I am not sure but my place at their table is the identical place I sat when I was a boy. Each of my siblings had "our place" at the table. Dad and Mama had their places. At the present table, a new one Steve had built, I can still see my Dad instructing us to hold hands while he prayed the only prayer I ever heard him pray: "Bless, O Lord, this food to our use and ourselves to thy service for Christ's sake. Amen."

When I drive along Redland Road and observe a new crop of corn growing beautifully I see my Dad. I see him in his old corn fields, admiring the fine ears of corn thriving on that rich Tallapoosa River bottomland. Some years those corn stalks towered over him and he would beam as he talked about the fine yield per acre he was expecting.

Though Dad left us 20 years ago he is still around. Only in my memories it's true. But memories are real. They are precious. And they do linger. Through their window I have seen my Dad a lot lately and I am blessed. +

58

Strength to run the race

The Boston Marathon made the news again. It was inspiring to see some runners who were injured in last year's bombing competing this time. Millions of us were cheering proudly for them.

Life is more like a marathon than a hundred-yard dash. Each of us must find the strength to get up every day – for a lifetime – and keep running. Stamina is an absolute necessity. Without perseverance we will not make it to the finish line. The race is not easy for anyone.

There is a biblical passage that speaks poignantly of this race. The writer of the Book of Hebrews admonishes us: "Let us run with perseverance the race marked out for us, fixing our eyes on Jesus, the pioneer and perfecter of faith" (NIV).

This admonition is found in the 12th chapter of Hebrews. What follows are some ideas that are helpful in our walk with the Lord. Read the first 12 verses of that chapter and then examine them with me:

1. We are surrounded by a great cloud of witnesses! We are not alone. Faithful servants of the past are alive in the Church Triumphant. Spiritually they are with us. They are in our balcony, cheering us on. Their presence inspires us to continue the race. In the stillness we can hear them shouting, "Go on! You can do it! Don't give up! Get up and go on!" This renews our hope and cheers us on.

2. We can run life's race with perseverance! We can do it but we cannot do it alone. We need help. That is where Jesus comes in. He is available. His strengthening presence can make the difference. We will stumble and fall sometimes but by looking to Jesus we can stay the course. Trails and misfortune can be overcome. We have Christ to guide us!

The hymn writer Fannie Crosby did not quit the race because of her blindness. After years of letting Christ lead her, she could write of the Savior's tender mercy and testify that he had "led her all the way." If we will only "look to Jesus" we can experience the same guidance and sing Fannie's song as our own:

Can I doubt His tender mercy,
Who through life has been my guide?
Heavenly peace, divinest comfort,
Here by faith in Him to dwell!
For I know, whate'er befall me,
Jesus doeth all things well;
For I know, whate'er befall me,
Jesus doeth all things well.

All the way my Savior leads me-
Cheers each winding path I tread,
Gives me grace for every trial,
Feeds me with the living bread.
Though my weary steps may falter
And my soul a-thirst may be,
Gushing from the Rock before me,
Lo! a spring of joy I see.

I love that song, especially the thought that Jesus "cheers each winding path I tread." He has! He does! He will!

3. Jesus endured the cross, shedding his own blood for our sins, and risen from the dead he has taken his seat at the right hand of the Father! Our suffering tempts us to doubt that God is in control of the world. The writer of Hebrews reminds us that Jesus did not die in vain; he endured the cross to fulfill the will of God. As Maltbie Babcock said, we must never forget that this is our Father's world, and "though the wrong seems oft so strong, God is the ruler yet"! Our hardships must not blind us to this reality.

4. Consider him so that you may not grow weary or lose heart! Indeed, consider Jesus! See him there, enduring the unbelievable pain of dying naked on a cross! In no way does our suffering compare to

his. When we remember that, the size of our own problems diminishes and we do not lose heart in the heat of the race. Consider the price Jesus paid for you and you will not "grow weary in doing well." You will simple give thanks – and walk on!

5. Humbly accept the trials of life because the Lord disciplines those whom he loves! Parents who do not discipline their children do not love their children. Authentic love includes discipline. Of course not every trial is sent from God. But some are. Because God loves us he "disciplines us for our good," that our lives may produce the fruit of righteousness. God is holy. He expects his children to be holy. His discipline helps us to "share his holiness." Holiness flows from submission and obedience. Holiness is not a "feeling" one gets from walking in a lovely sanctuary; it is Christ "made flesh" again in the way we live the common life.

6. Lift your drooping hands, strengthen your weak knees, and walk straight with your feet! In light of what Christ has done, we must stand on our feet! The sacrificial work of Jesus is enough to inspire us to lift our hands in praise to God. Our Savior's love motivates us to become strong in our witness, bold in our service, and morally straight in everyday living. When we "stand up for Jesus" our lameness is miraculously healed by the grace of God.

7. Jesus goes before us as our pioneer leader. He is the author and perfecter of our faith. Faith in God makes sense because of Jesus. Jesus is our faith. Apart from him there is no Christian faith. He is the core of faith, the source of faith. He is our model of obedience to God. Jesus could endure the cross because he knew the Father's joy awaited him. We also can endure trials for the joy awaiting us.

When his presence dwells within us we can run life's race with perseverance that honors our Lord and brings us at last to spiritual maturity. The key is to keep looking to Jesus as our leader and guide. The faithful saints of the ages did that and we can too! Christ is our Leader. He is out in front of us, beckoning us to follow him. Whatever it takes, we must not falter! +

59

Jonah and the whale

Some of the best stories ever written are scattered through the book popularly known as "the good book." The Bible contains stories of romance, intrigue, murder, wars, shipwrecks, suicide and adventure.

Even pagans and agnostics can have fun reading the Bible. You don't have to believe that it is the greatest book ever written to enjoy its fascinating stories of human struggle, failure and achievement.

One of my favorite stories is that of Jonah and the whale. That story has had such an impact upon the world that the very word "Jonah" brings us the image of the whale. But when you read the story, no whale is mentioned. Instead it is a "fish" that swallows Jonah. Was the fish a whale? What do you think?

Here is where some people stumble. They reason that even if a big fish could swallow a man, the man could not possibly survive the ordeal. They conclude then that this is not a real story, but one like the tale of Jack and the Bean Stalk. This conclusion is one option but the significance of the Jonah story does not hinge on whether you believe that a big fish could swallow a man.

The Jonah story offers some delightful observations. The fish obeyed God when Jonah did not. God "commanded" the fish to vomit Jonah out of his belly on land. Jonah, however, was at sea because he was running from God. God had commanded Jonah to go to Nineveh but Jonah ran the other way.

Running, then, may not be the great exercise that health experts believe it is. It could be hazardous to your future, and to your health, especially if you are running from God.

The best chuckle Jonah gives us is this: even a fish cannot stomach a backslider for more than three days before it becomes sick of him. I will leave it to you to ask your own pastor if backsliders cause preachers to be nauseated. Or you can draw your own conclusion.

All chuckles aside, in many ways the story of Jonah is the story of every person. Look at the sequence of events. God called. Jonah ran. Jonah was miserable. God showed mercy. Jonah stopped running and obeyed God. Then things got better for Jonah.

Is that not much like our own experience? God calls. We run. We are miserable. God shows us mercy. Then, if we are wise, we respond to God's mercy by obeying him. Otherwise our story will likely have a sad ending.

I have often compared my own life to that of Jonah. Not that a big fish ever swallowed me but for years I stayed busy thinking up excuses for not obeying God.

God called me to preach when I was in my teens, still in high school. But I doubted. I ran. I tried to write my own ticket in college. But I was miserable. Only when I surrendered to God's call and stopped running did I find peace. Ever since then I have pleaded for sufficient grace to continue to obey God. In his mercy God gave me blessed assurance about my mission in life.

Our oldest son Matt heard God call. Like Jonah he ran, and he even ran to the sea. He spent 10 years in the Navy. He saw the world but in no port did he find peace because all those years he was running from God.

God's mercy finally overwhelmed Matt's misery. Like Jonah he gave up and began to obey God. You could have knocked me over with a feather when he told me, "Dad, I think God is calling me to preach." In my great wisdom I tried to talk him out of it. I told him that God needs Christian men in every arena of life. He listened patiently and then asked, "But, Dad, what if God really is calling me to preach?" I replied, "Then, son, you had better do what God wants you to do." Matt got busy, completed college and then entered seminary.

He finished seminary at age 44. Like Jonah Matt found peace by obeying God. Is Matt a late bloomer? You might think so. Matt says, "I believe I was on God's time table, right on schedule."

Bible stories are useful for much more than Vacation Bible

Schools. We can learn from biblical stories much about God and much about ourselves. I reckon that's why I love the story of Jonah so much. I could identify with Jonah. And I learned a powerful lesson from his story. I learned that I could never have peace with God while running and making excuses – that peace only comes through obeying God.

When I get to heaven, Jonah will be one of the first fellows I want to chat with. And I want to find out just how big that fish really was! +

60

The baptism of Laurida Emily

Across my years of ministry many young parents have asked me to "christen" their new baby. Though "christening" actually refers to the giving of a Christian name to a child, among Christians the word is synonymous with "baptism." Like most pastors I consider it an honor to arrange for the baptism or christening of a child.

Methodists, like many other Christian communions, practice infant baptism. I respect those who chose not to baptize infants. My Baptist friends do not but prefer to help parents "dedicate" a new baby to the Lord. And of course the dedication of a child to the Lord is both biblical and beautiful.

We Methodists go a step beyond "dedication" by believing that through infant baptism the child has been "initiated" into the Church. Baptism is the doorway of entry into the body of Christ.

Baptism does not make an infant a Christian or what we call a "professing member" of the church. That will require a decision later by the child who, having been nurtured in the faith by parents and the church, will accept God's grace for themselves and become "a full and responsible member of Christ's holy Church." This decision is what we call a person's "confirmation" in the faith.

On a recent Sunday I had the extraordinary honor of baptizing an infant who was given the name of my deceased sister, Laurida Emily. As a young pastor I was privileged to perform the marriage of Laurida to Dick Berkstresser in our parents' home. Laurida and Dick were blessed with seven children, the youngest being Margaret Emily. Margaret and her husband Keith Krawczynski asked me to baptize their infant daughter, Laurida Emily, in the early worship service at Mulder United Methodist Church near Wetumpka.

Other Books by Walter Albritton

If You Want to Walk on Water,
You've Got to Get Out of Your Boat

233 Days
God hurts like you hurt when death claims someone you love

Life is Short
So Laugh Often, Live Fully and Love Deeply

Just Get Over It and Move On!

Don't Let Go of the Rope!

The Four Gospels
(Commentary on Selected Passages)

Paul's Letters
(Commentary on Selected Passages)

Beacons of Hope
(Commentary on Selected New Testament Passages)

Do the Best You Can
With What You've Got, Where You Are, While There's Time

You Simply Can't Trust a Talking Bird

Leaning Over the Banisters of Heaven
(Balcony People Make the Difference)

+++

pledged to nurture her in the faith as she grows up. The church entered into a covenant with Keith and Margaret to assist this child to grow in grace and one day affirm Christ as her Savior and Lord. The lay leader of the church, Jenny Hamilton, led the congregation in affirming this covenant.

In the presence of a lively congregation of believers I prayed that the Lord would guide Laurida Emily's parents and the church to help her grow up to know, love and serve the Lord Jesus Christ. I believe that is a prayer the Lord will gladly answer.

The baptism of a baby – is it just another routine ritual of the church? Heavens no! It is a magnificent experience of the grace of God! Glory! +

The baptism of this little girl, the granddaughter of my dear sister, was deeply emotional for me. I took the liberty of singing a verse of Laurida's favorite song, "Shall we gather at the river." With other members of my family I was remembering the raucous laughter of Laurida and giving thanks to God for her infectious enthusiasm for life.

Twenty years ago Laurida went home to the Father's House – all too soon it seemed to us who loved her. But while we wish she was still with us we have learned to yield to God's sovereignty by saying, "The Lord gives, and the Lord takes away; blessed be the name of the Lord."

During the baptismal ceremony I presented Keith, Laurida Emily's father, with a "Clinging Cross." I told him it was a gift for the baby but asked him to care for it until the Lord told him it was the right time to give it to his daughter. The little brown cross is a simple thing, small enough to hold in one hand. A card with it explains that it is not a magic piece but when you cling to it, it reminds you of the nail-scarred hands of the One who died upon the cross for our sins. When I hold that little cross in my hand I remember the song that says, "The cross upon which Jesus died is a shelter in which we may hide."

What happened to Laurida Emily as I baptized her? I don't know. She was actually asleep most of the time. Then she woke up, yawned and looked around as though she was wondering what was going on. Did she experience the grace of God? I believe so since God is not limited by our understanding or perception. I believe God put his hand upon her even as her pastor Mark Jackson and I put our hands upon her in the act of baptism with water.

There is nothing magical about baptism. We pastors do what we do but we do not control God. It is entirely possible that in the sacrament of baptism God works in the small heart of a child in ways we do not understand. The water is symbolic of God's cleansing power of the human heart. The amount of water used has no bearing on the efficacy of baptism. For that reason we Methodists allow people to choose any of the three typical modes of baptism: immersion, pouring or sprinkling.

What I do know about Laurida Emily's baptism is that her parents presented her to the Lord in the holy sacrament of baptism and